Research Report

Results from the Teach For America 2015 National Principal Survey

Mollie Rudnick, Amanda F Edelman, Ujwal Kharel, Matthew W. Lewis

Sponsored by Teach For America

RAND CORPORATION

For more information on this publication, visit www.rand.org/t/rr1116

Library of Congress Cataloging-in-Publication Data

is available for this publication.

ISBN: 978-0-8330-9166-6

Published by the RAND Corporation, Santa Monica, Calif.

Preface

Teach For America's (TFA's) mission is to build the movement to eliminate educational inequity by developing leaders for U.S. schools who are committed to providing to low-income children the same access to a great education that their wealthier peers have (TFA, undated). This 2015 principal survey is the tenth in a series to provide answers regarding how TFA is doing in providing high-quality, appropriately prepared corps members to schools in an effort to support and improve progress toward this mission. The results of this survey are provided in this report and show the context and conditions in which corps members are working, how principals perceive corps members, and how principals perceive their interactions with TFA. These findings offer insights that TFA staff can consider as they try to provide more-tailored supports to corps members, inform professional development to meet the needs of corps members and the schools they staff, and continue to build relationships with the principals of schools in which corps members serve.

TFA contracted with researchers in RAND Education, a division of the RAND Corporation, to conduct this research.

Contents

Figures

Tables

Summary

More than 1,800 principals across the United States who work with Teach For America (TFA) corps members completed this year's National Principal Survey, for an overall response rate of 54 percent. TFA seeks to build the movement to eliminate educational inequity by developing leaders (corps members) who teach for a two-year commitment in low-income schools. As was the case with previous survey results, the findings from this survey show that principals value the contributions that corps members, alumni, and TFA make to their schools:

- Respondents and their schools shared some common characteristics.
  - Respondents had an average of five years in the role of principal, with experience in this role ranging from zero to 40 years. On average, respondents had less experience than all U.S. principals.[1]
  - Seventy-one percent of participants lead traditional public schools, followed in frequency by charter schools (27 percent), early-childhood education centers (5 percent), private schools (1 percent), and schools managed by the national Bureau of Indian Education (1 percent).
- Respondents reported high levels of satisfaction with TFA corps members.
  - The majority of responding principals (81 percent) indicated that they were satisfied with the corps members at their schools.
- Respondents had generally positive feedback about corps members.
  - More than 60 percent of principals agreed that corps members made a positive impact on their schools in the areas of academic achievement, classroom culture, relationships with parents, school culture and faculty collaboration, and socioemotional development.
  - The majority of participants indicated that corps members were equally or more proficient than other novice teachers at their schools across a range of skills, including developing positive relationships with colleagues and administrators, having high expectations for all students, and having a high impact on student performance.
  - More than 60 percent of principals considered corps members' level of involvement in school activities (e.g., sponsoring student groups, coaching sports, serving on school- and district-wide task forces) to be typical of involvement for other novice teachers.
  - Although there was no significant difference between principal or school characteristics and overall satisfaction with corps members, principals who were TFA

---

[1] The nationally representative sample of principals responding to the 2012 national Schools and Staffing Survey indicated they had 12 years of experience (National Center for Education Statistics, 2014).

alumni and those who led charter schools were significantly less likely to report positive feelings about corps members. On the other hand, principals with more years of experience teaching and those with more years of experience as principals were significantly more likely to report positive feelings about corps members.

- Respondents were willing to hire or recommend hiring corps members.
  - Eighty-six percent of responding principals indicated that they would be willing to hire another TFA corps member if they had a teaching vacancy at their school.
  - Most participants (66 percent) responded that they "definitely would recommend" hiring a corps member to a fellow school leader.
  - About half of principals identified classroom management (50 percent) and the fact that corps members teach for only a two-year commitment (57 percent) as reasons they would not hire additional corps members. More principals identified all other factors (e.g., teaching ability, content knowledge, support and training provided by TFA, commitment to teaching, and experiences with previous corps members) as reasons they would hire additional corps members (versus reasons they would not hire them).
- Respondents had positive feedback about TFA's support.
  - Eighty-seven percent of principals indicated that they were satisfied with the support TFA provides corps members.
  - More than three-quarters of participants indicated that the support that corps members receive complements their schools' induction or training "to some extent" or "to a great extent."
- Principals reported positive feelings about alumni working in their schools.
  - Just over half of respondents indicated that TFA alumni worked at their schools.
  - More than 80 percent of principals felt that the alumni working in their schools made a positive contribution to their schools in a variety of areas.

Abbreviations

NCES	National Center for Education Statistics
SASS	Schools and Staffing Survey
TFA	Teach For America

Chapter One. Introduction

This report outlines the findings from the administration of the 2015 National Principal Survey to principals in schools serving Teach For America (TFA) corps members. TFA seeks to build the movement to eliminate educational inequity by developing leaders (corps members) who teach for a two-year commitment in low-income schools. This survey seeks to understand how TFA is doing in providing high-quality, appropriately prepared corps members to schools in an effort to support and improve progress toward its mission. The introduction provides an overview of the survey process, demographic information about the survey respondents, and descriptions of the respondents' schools. Chapter Two covers satisfaction with corps members, satisfaction with the support that TFA provides, comparisons of survey findings across principal and school characteristics, and satisfaction with TFA alumni. The document concludes with four appendixes:

- Appendix A: significance-test results
- Appendix B: the overall responses for each question
- Appendix C: the responses broken out by alumni status
- Appendix D: the responses broken out by charter and non–charter school status.

Survey Administration

In the fall of 2014, TFA contracted with the RAND Corporation to administer the 2015 National Principal Survey. TFA provided us with a spreadsheet of schools at which TFA corps members were employed during the 2014–2015 school year and the contact information for the principals at those schools. We administered the survey using an online interface between January and April 2015. TFA is divided into 50 regional offices that work directly with schools and corps members in each region. TFA regional staff sent an introductory email notifying principals of the upcoming survey, followed by an email from RAND that provided the principals with a link to the survey. The regional staff also sent biweekly reminder emails to principals, as needed, to encourage them to complete the survey. Email addresses were not available for 25 principals across 12 of the regions; those principals did not receive the survey.

Response Rates

Of the 3,338 principals identified as having corps members and email addresses, 1,803 responded to the online survey, for an overall response rate of 54 percent. In at least six cases, someone other than the principal who was familiar with TFA corps members at the school completed the survey (e.g., assistant principal or dean of instruction). Regional response rates ranged from 39 percent to 100 percent. Table 1.1 displays the number of schools in each TFA region and their response rates.

Table 1.1. Survey Sample and Response Rate, by Region

Region	Number of Schools in the Region	Percentage of Principals Responding
Alabama	46	39
Appalachia	20	60
Arkansas	37	57
Baltimore	103	50
Bay Area	164	42
Buffalo	8	63
Charlotte	37	46
Chicago	191	54
Colorado	85	60
Connecticut	80	51
D.C. Region	76	58
Dallas–Fort Worth	91	60
Delaware	19	74
Detroit	75	49
Eastern North Carolina	98	68
Greater Nashville	73	52
Greater New Orleans–Louisiana Delta	89	48
Greater Philadelphia	45	40
Hawaii	43	72
Houston	108	52
Indianapolis	45	58
Jacksonville	43	70
Kansas City	37	38
Las Vegas Valley	52	63
Los Angeles	91	47
Massachusetts	66	50
Memphis	109	48
Metro Atlanta	91	48
Miami–Dade	40	68
Milwaukee	58	71
Mississippi	73	45
New Jersey	79	44
New Mexico	40	48

Region	Number of Schools in the Region	Percentage of Principals Responding
New York	289	44
North Carolina Piedmont Triad	15	100
Northeast Ohio–Cleveland	43	53
Oklahoma	93	67
Phoenix	88	55
Rhode Island	20	100
Rio Grande Valley	71	56
Sacramento	18	61
San Antonio	76	53
San Diego	15	67
South Carolina	79	72
South Dakota	20	40
South Louisiana	42	52
Southwest Ohio	34	59
St. Louis	57	58
Twin Cities	26	65
Washington	40	48
Overall (total number; mean percentage)	3,338	54

The overall response rate was lower than the rate for the 2013 survey, which was 66 percent. The low response rate, in general and compared with the 2013 survey, can be attributed to several reasons. The response rate was likely lower than the 2013 survey because established agreements on safeguards for confidentiality did not allow us to provide TFA with a list of principals who had not yet completed the survey. Thus, TFA regional offices could not provide targeted follow-up to principals to increase survey response rates. Although the TFA regional offices sent general emails to all principals reminding them to complete the survey, there is evidence to suggest that personalized correspondence is a more-effective means of facilitating survey responses (Cook, Heath, and Thompson, 2000; Rose, Sidle, and Griffith, 2007). Additionally, the response rate might have been low in general because of changes in school staffing and the fact that the most up-to-date information on principals and their contact information were not always available. In some cases, emailed principals no longer worked at the schools; in other cases, schools included on the list from TFA did not have corps members currently working there. In both instances, we became aware of the changes only if the principals notified us. Another possible explanation for the generally low response rate might have been large numbers of undelivered emails in certain school districts, indicating that district spam filters might have stopped the survey emails. Thus, it is not clear whether all principals actually received the email invitations and survey links. Finally, evidence suggests that survey response rates (whether paper or electronic) have historically been declining since the 1970s, stabilizing to around 49 percent between the mid-1990s and 2005 (Baruch and Holtom, 2008; Baruch, 1999). This level of response is consistent with the response rate achieved during the administration of this survey.

Limitations

The results reported here are limited to the principals who completed the survey. Furthermore, the survey asked principals to report their overall opinions about TFA corps members at their schools. In cases in which principals had multiple corps members at their schools, they might have had very different opinions about individual corps members, making it difficult to provide a single overall response.

Characteristics of Responding Principals

We asked participating principals to provide demographic information, including information about their experiences in the field of education, an estimation of the amount of time spent on the tasks to which they attend as principal, and their role in the teacher-hiring process. Although TFA focuses on high-need schools and does not seek to serve a nationally representative set of schools, we compare the characteristics of respondents with those of principals nationally to give a sense of the representativeness of the responding principals. To do so, we report data from a nationally representative sample of principals who completed the National Center for Education Statistics (NCES) 2011–2012 national Schools and Staffing Survey (SASS) (NCES, 2014).

Demographics

Respondents to the 2015 National Principal Survey were more likely to identify as female, as black or African American, as an "other" race, or as Hispanic than the 2011–2012 SASS respondents. Table 1.2 shows the demographics of respondents to the 2015 TFA National Principal Survey and the 2011–2012 SASS respondents.

Table 1.2. Comparison of Demographics for 2015 Teach For America Survey Respondents and 2011–2012 Schools and Staffing Survey Principals

Demographics	Percentage of 2015 Responding Principals	Percentage of 2011–2012 SASS Principals[a]
Female	63	52
American Indian or Native Alaskan	2	1
Asian	3	1
Black or African American	38	10
Native Hawaiian or other Pacific Islander	0	0
Other	7	0
White	54	88
Hispanic	14	6

[a] From NCES, 2014.

Work Experience

When compared with the nationwide sample of SASS respondents, who averaged 12 years of teaching experience and nearly eight years of principal experience, responding principals overseeing TFA corps members generally had fewer years of experience working in these capacities (NCES, 2014). Prior to becoming principals, the majority of respondents to the 2015 National Principal Survey had either zero to five years (27 percent) or six to ten years of elementary or secondary teaching experience (39 percent), with an average of approximately ten years of teaching experience. As seen in Figure 1.1, nearly half of responding principals had three or fewer years of experience in the role of principal, with an average of five years of experience serving as a principal. Additionally, 87 percent of respondents indicated that they previously served in other school administrative roles, such as assistant principal, vice principal, or dean.

Figure 1.1. Principals' Years of Experience as Principals

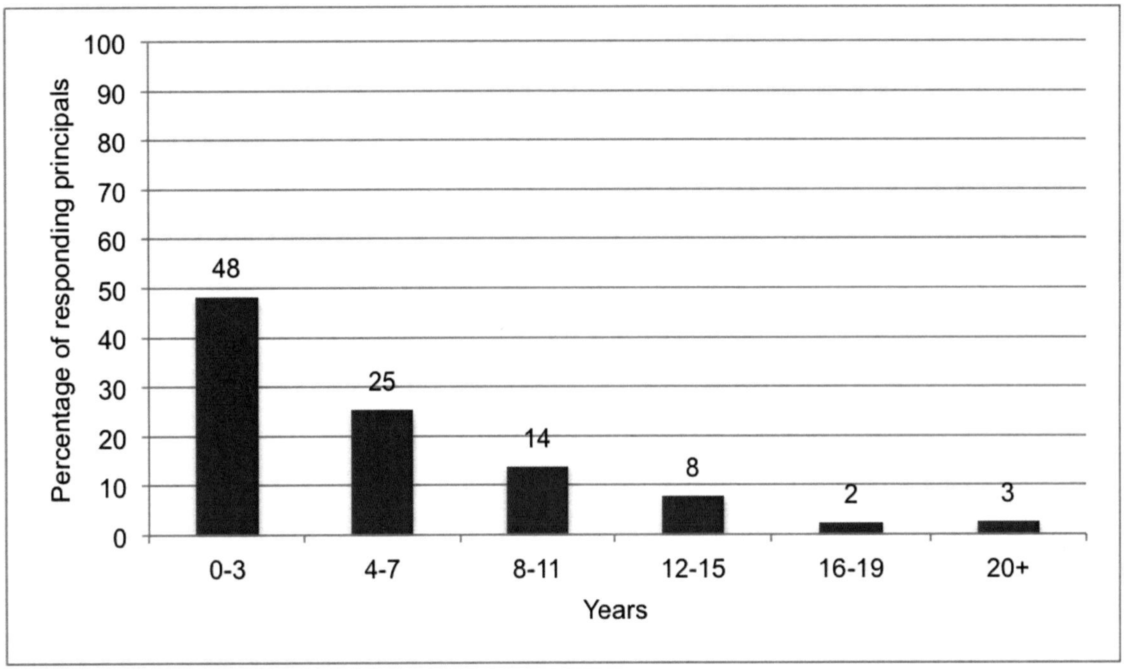

Seventy-six percent of respondents reported that they had worked with TFA corps members while serving in the role of principal for two or more years. These findings seem to indicate that most of the survey's respondents had been working with corps members for their entire careers as principals. Finally, 12 percent of respondents reported being TFA alumni. This is comparable to the findings from the 2013 National Principal Survey, in which 11 percent of respondents reported being TFA alumni (McCann, Turner, and White, 2013).

Role in the Hiring Process

Ninety-three percent of respondents reported that they had "major involvement" in making decisions concerning the hiring of new full-time teachers at their schools (see Table 1.3).

Table 1.3. Involvement in the Hiring of New Full-Time Teachers

Involvement	Percentage of Principals Responding (*N* = 1,697)
Major	93
Moderate	5
Minor	1
No	1

Eighty-two percent of participants indicated that they participated in interviewing TFA corps members. When SASS participants were asked about the amount of influence they had on hiring new full-time teachers at their schools, 84 percent indicated that they had "major influence," and nearly 10 percent indicated that they had "moderate influence" (NCES, 2014).

Characteristics of School Sites

We also asked participating principals to provide information describing their schools.

School Description

The characteristics of respondents' schools were generally similar to those found in past administrations of the TFA National Principal Survey. Principals reported having up to 95 full-time–equivalent teachers working under them, with an average school size of 25 full-time–equivalent teachers. Data provided by TFA's survey contact list indicate that 32 percent of respondents' schools have one corps member (see Figure 1.2). This is a slight increase over the results of the 2013 National Principal Survey, in which 27 percent of principals reported having one corps member at their schools (McCann, Turner, and White, 2013). Other responses about the number of corps members employed in a school were fairly consistent with the 2013 National Principal Survey findings (McCann, Turner, and White, 2013).

Figure 1.2. Number of Corps Members per School

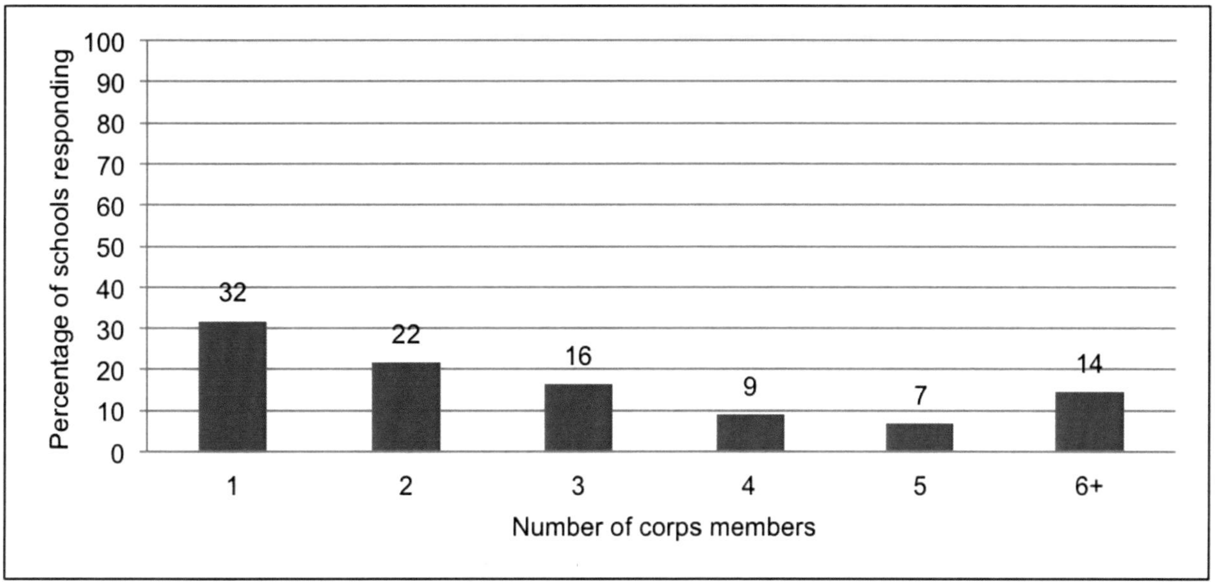

SOURCE: TFA.

We asked principals to indicate whether their schools were charter schools, early-childhood education centers, managed by the Bureau of Indian Education, or private schools. We assumed that any principal indicating no to all four questions led a traditional public school (see Figure 1.3). Approximately 1 percent of principals selected multiple options, indicating that their schools fell into more than one category (e.g., early-childhood education charter school). Charter schools were overrepresented in the 2015 National Principal Survey. Although 27 percent of respondents to the 2015 National Principal Survey were charter school principals, charter schools made up only 6.2 percent of schools in the nation in 2012–2013 (NCES, undated).

Figure 1.3. School Governance Structures

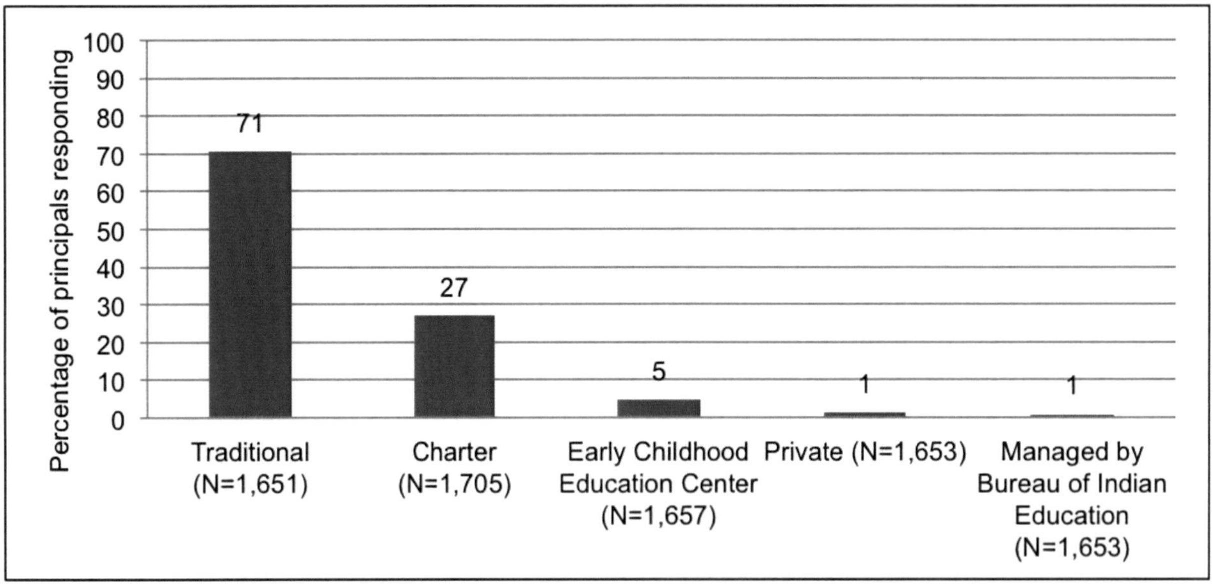

NOTE: We calculated the percentage of traditional schools from respondents who answered all four questions about school type (*N* = 1,651) in the negative.

Finally, when asked whether teachers are given a common planning time, 94 percent of survey participants answered in the affirmative. Just under 73 percent of SASS respondents answered in the affirmative when asked a similar question about whether teachers have a common planning time for professional development (NCES, 2014). This suggests that a higher proportion of TFA survey respondents provide common planning time that could allow for an opportunity for teachers to collaborate, communicate, and provide feedback on each other's work to improve practice.

In sum, principals reporting in this survey were generally similar to a nationally representative sample of principals who responded to the 2011–2012 SASS, except that principals who responded to the 2015 TFA survey had less experience as teachers and as principals and were more racially and ethnically diverse than the SASS principals. Similar proportions of principals reporting to the 2015 and 2013 TFA surveys were corps alumni themselves. Chapter Two focuses on principals' perceptions about current TFA corps members and whether school and principals' characteristics are related to those perceptions.

Chapter Two. Survey Findings About Corps Members, Alumni, and Teach For America

This chapter reports findings on respondents' overall satisfaction with corps members, along with reasons contributing to that satisfaction (e.g., corps members' skills, impact on the school environment, or school involvement), and whether the principal would hire a new corps member or recommend that colleagues do so. After reporting on the overall trends, we look at findings for a variety of subgroups. As detailed below, principals were generally satisfied with corps members, and those feelings were reflected in their responses about hiring additional corps members.

Principal Satisfaction with Corps Members Was Generally High

When asked about the extent to which they agreed with the statement, "I am satisfied with the Teach For America corps members in my school," the majority of respondents (81 percent) answered in the affirmative. This is fairly consistent with the findings from the 2013 National Principal Survey, in which 94 percent of respondents indicated that they "strongly agreed" or "moderately agreed" with the statement of overall satisfaction (McCann, Turner, and White, 2013). However, 20 percent of this year's respondents disagreed with the statement (see Figure 2.1), a large increase from the 2013 survey, which found that 6 percent of respondents disagreed with the statement about overall satisfaction with corps members.

Figure 2.1. Principals' Overall Levels of Satisfaction with Corps Members

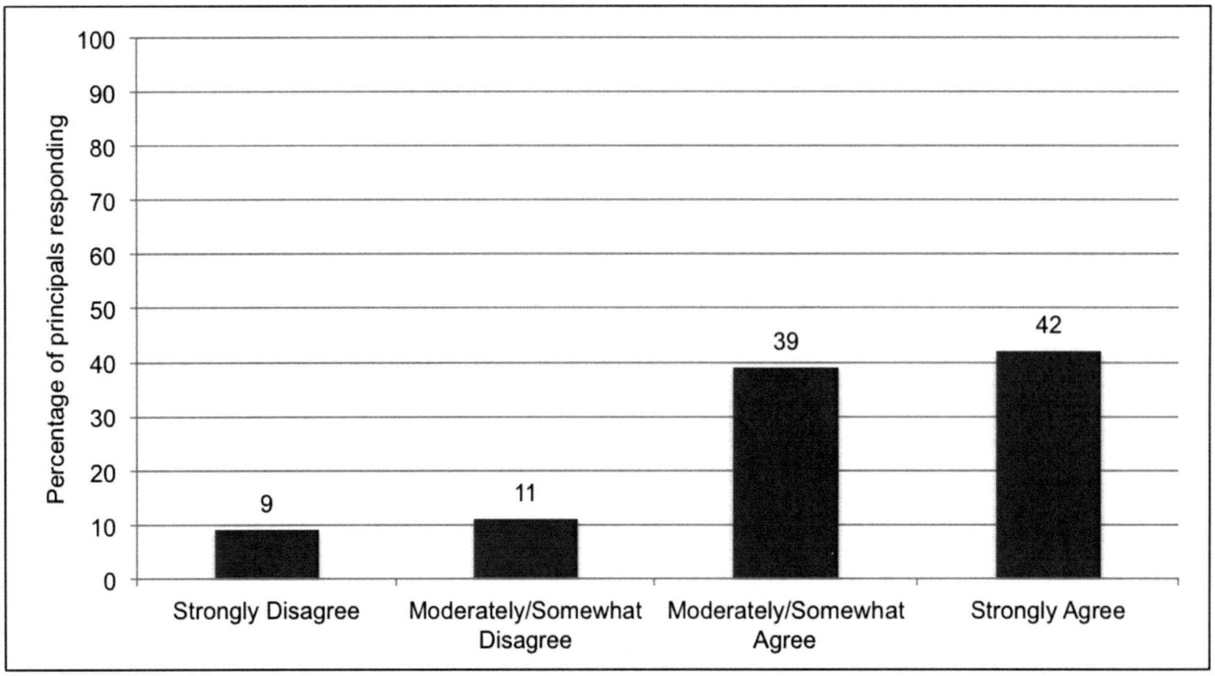

NOTE: The numbers do not sum to 100 because of rounding.

Factors Potentially Contributing to Principal Satisfaction with Corps Members

Five of the survey questions sought to better understand principals' perceptions of corps members.

Principals Reported That Corps Members Make a Positive Difference in a Variety of Areas

We asked principals to indicate whether corps members make a positive, negative, or no difference in a variety of areas. As Figure 2.2 illustrates, the majority of respondents indicated that TFA corps members made positive contributions in all five areas.

Figure 2.2. Principals' Perceptions of the Difference Corps Members Make

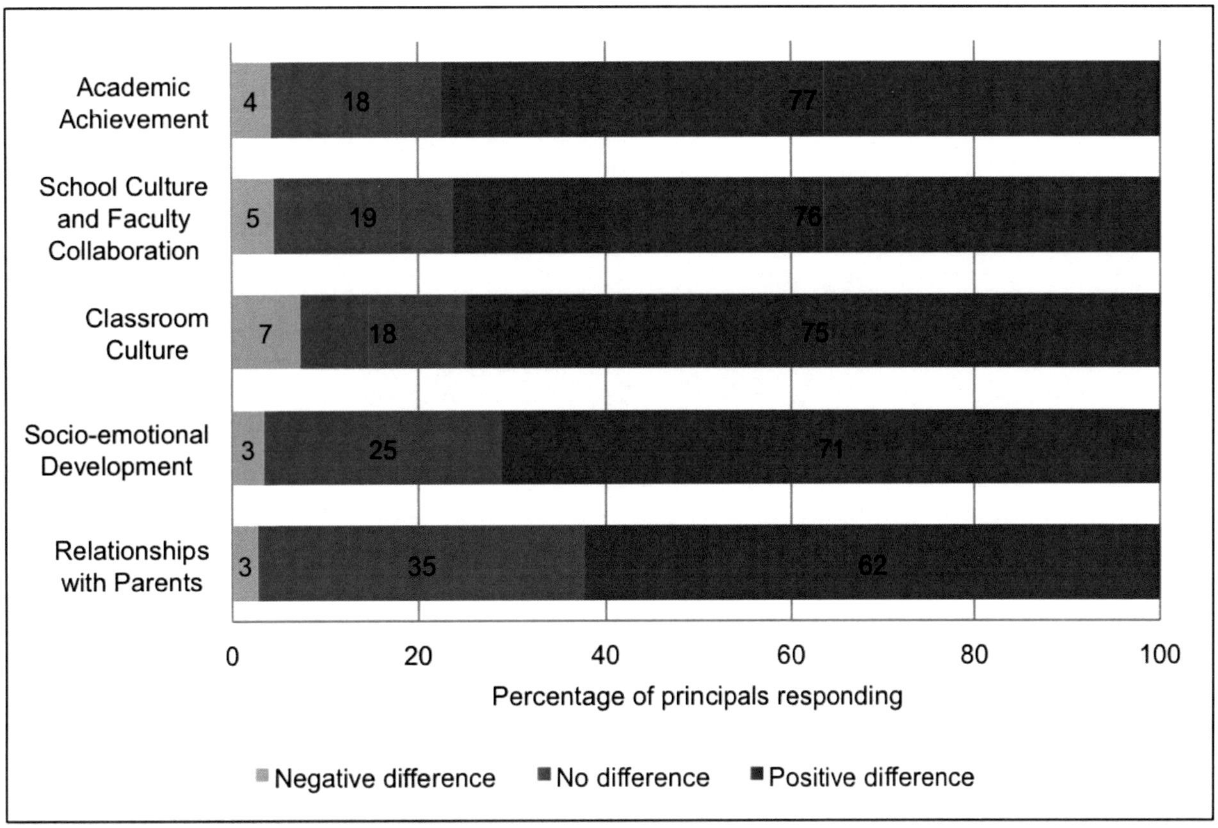

Principals Reported That Corps Members Possess a Variety of Skills

We also asked principals to rate corps members on eight skills and indicate how corps members' skills compared with those of other novice teachers with less than two years of teaching experience at their schools. Respondents generally rated corps members highly on all skills. As seen in Figure 2.3, the vast majority of respondents felt that corps members' skills were good, very good, or excellent in all areas. Additionally, more than 60 percent of respondents felt that corps members' abilities to develop positive relationships with colleagues and administrators and to have high expectations for all students were very good or excellent.

Figure 2.3. Principals' Ratings of Corps Members' Abilities

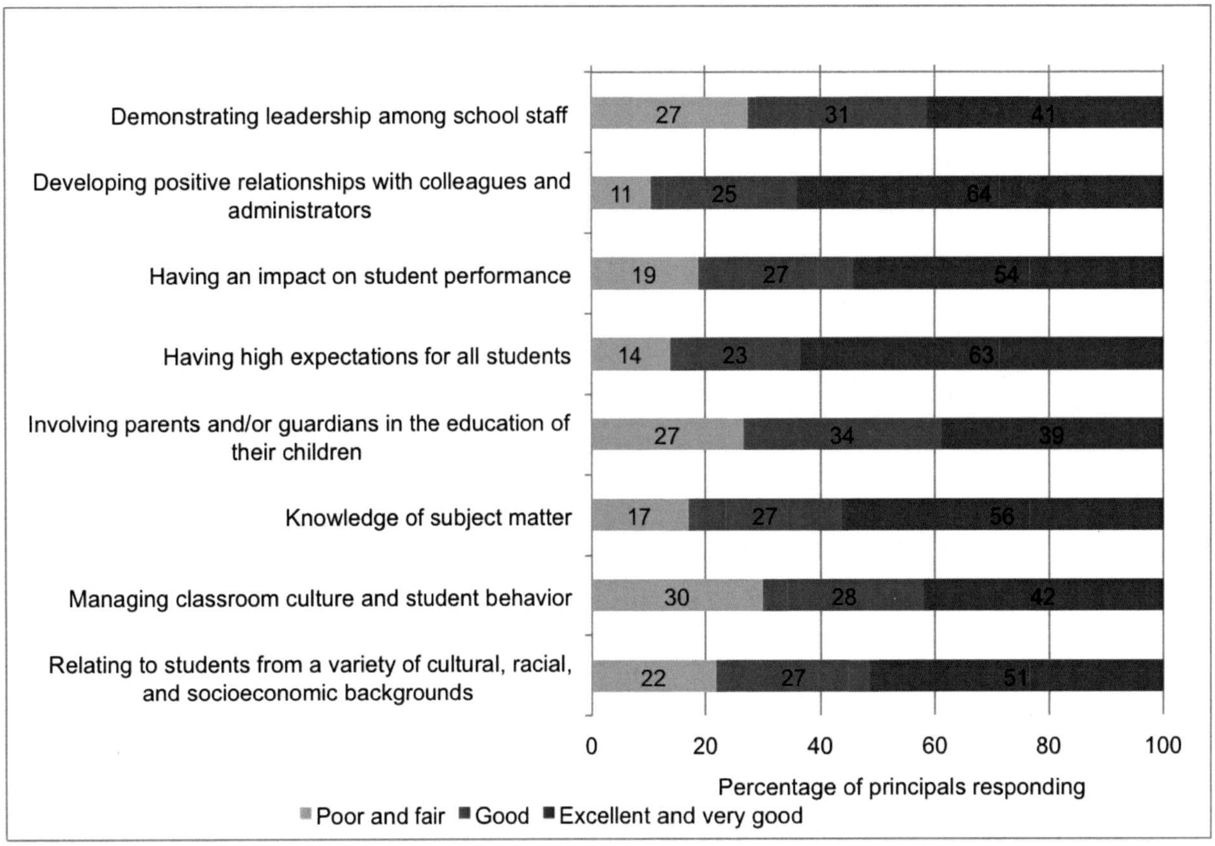

As shown in Figure 2.4, most principals responded that TFA corps members were "the same," "somewhat more proficient," or "much more proficient" than other novice teachers. Respondents generally selected affirmative and neutral responses at similar rates; a minority of respondents indicated that corps members were "somewhat less proficient" or "less proficient" than other novice teachers. A majority felt that TFA corps members were more proficient than other novice teachers at having an impact on student performance and having high expectations for students. A majority also reported that corps members and other novice teachers were similar in their abilities to involve parents and guardians in the education of their children.

Figure 2.4. Principals' Perceptions of Corps Members' Abilities Compared with Those of Other Novice Teachers

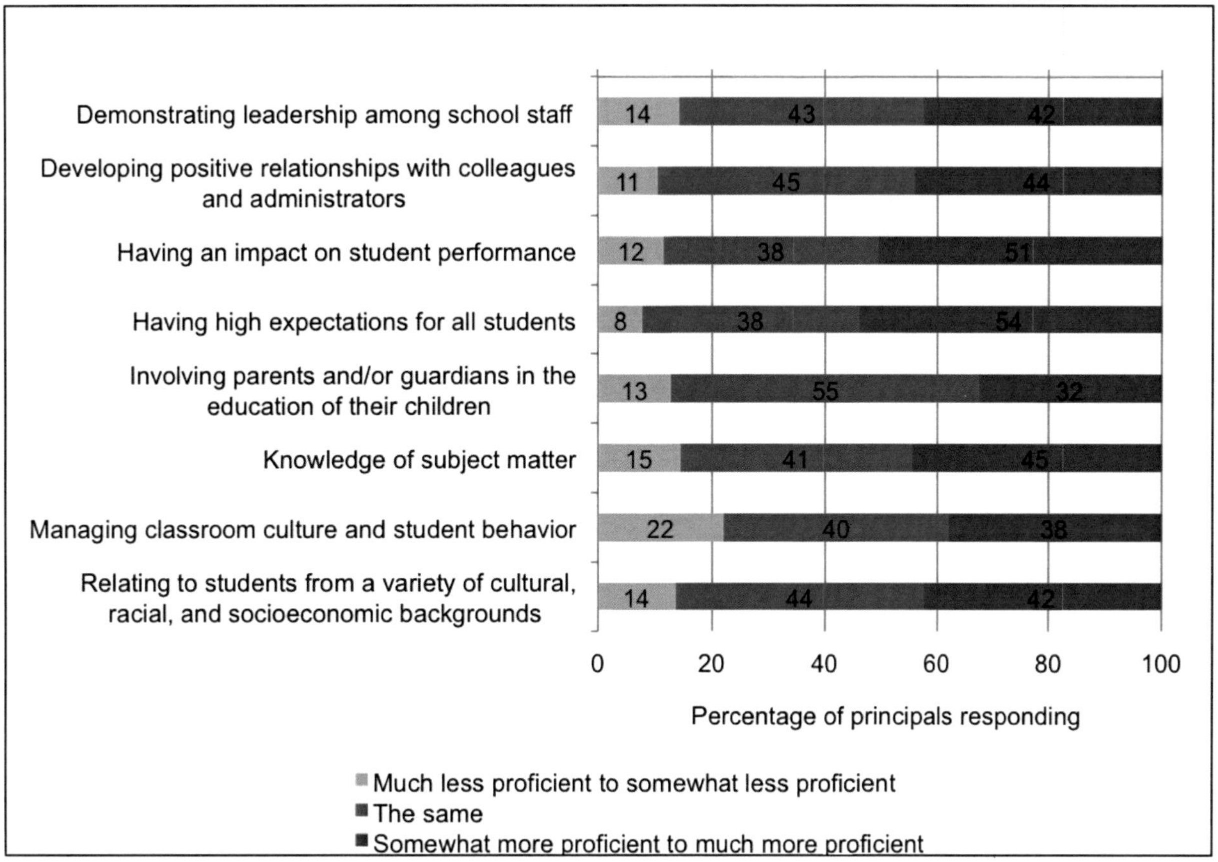

Principals Reported That Corps Members Made Contributions Outside the Classroom at a Level Similar to That of Other Novice Teachers

We asked respondents to indicate the proportion of corps members involved in school activities outside the classroom and compare the rates at which corps members and other novice teachers are involved. As shown in Figure 2.5, 62 percent of principals said that some or all corps members participated in sponsoring student groups, and 55 percent reported that they served on committees. For the remainder of the activities listed, a majority of principals reported that no corps members participated in the given activity. As shown in Figure 2.6, most principals considered these levels of corps members' participation to be similar to that of other novice teachers.

Figure 2.5. Principals' Perceptions of Corps Members' Participation in School Activities

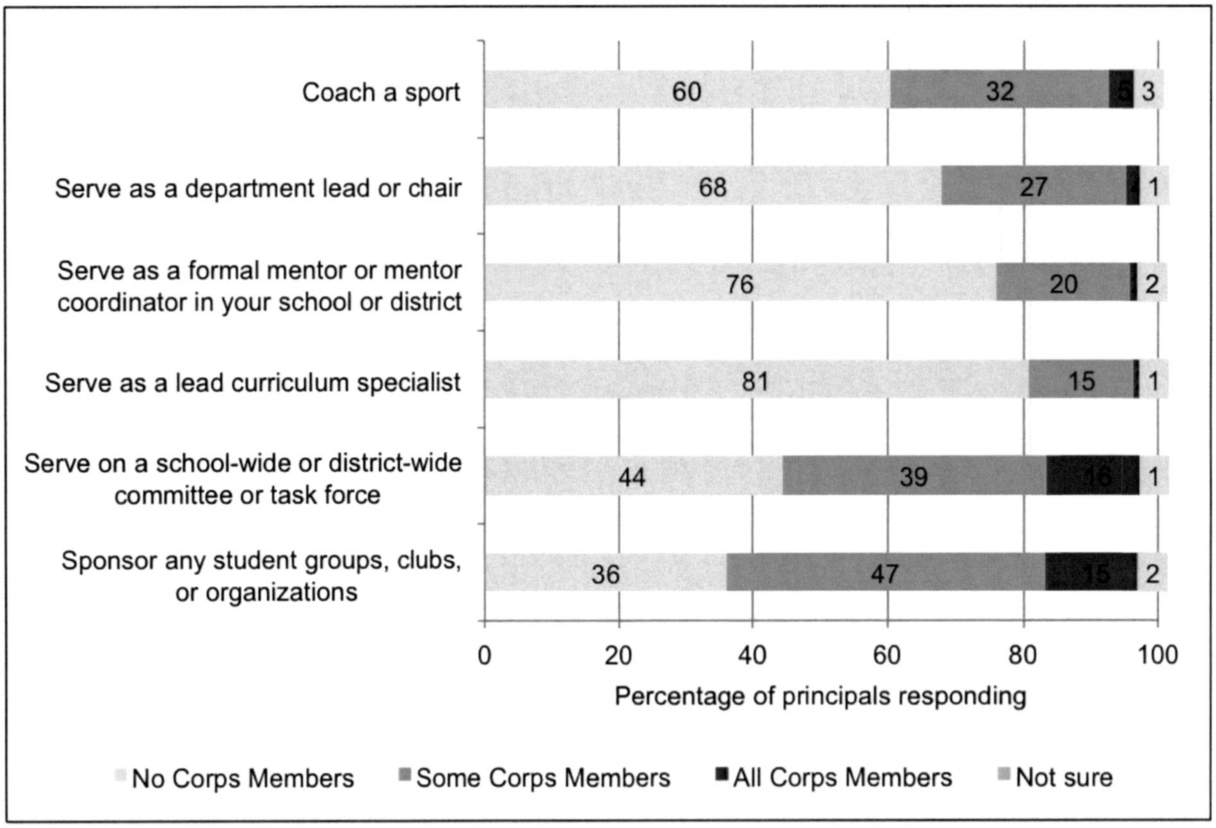

Figure 2.6. Principals' Perceptions of Corps Members' Participation in School Activities Compared with That of Other Novice Teachers

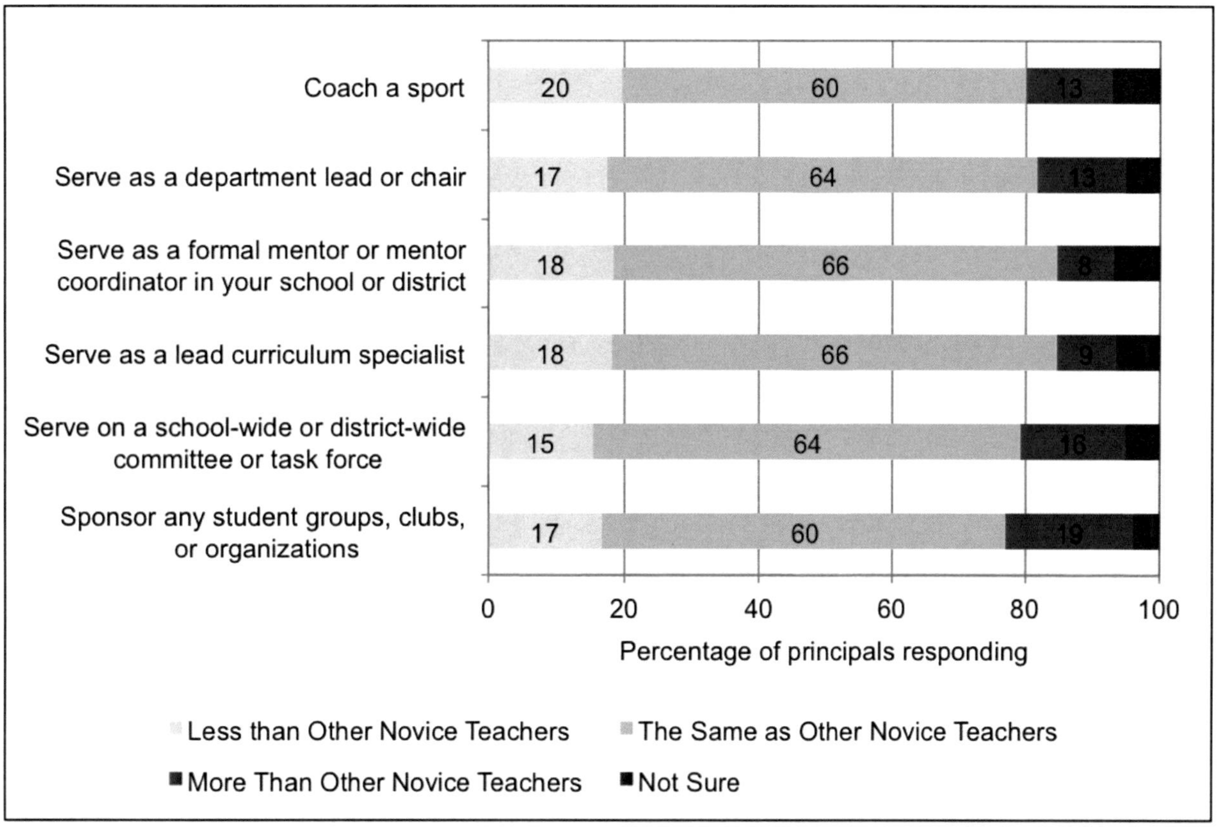

Most Principals Reported Willingness to Hire or Recommend Hiring Corps Members in the Future

In another series of questions, we asked principals whether they would hire TFA corps members in the future for job openings at their schools and whether they would recommend hiring corps members to a colleague. The majority of respondents indicated that they would be willing to hire corps members to fill teaching vacancies (86 percent). This result is consistent with the responses to the administration of the 2013 National Principal Survey, on which 84 percent of participants responded that they would hire corps members to fill teaching vacancies. Further, most participants (66 percent) in this year's survey indicated that they would "definitely" recommend hiring corps members to other principals. This is higher than in the 2013 National Principal Survey, in which only 49 percent of respondents indicated that they were "extremely likely" to recommend the hiring of corps members to other principals. Although most principals said that they would hire corps members to fill vacancies, fewer said that they would recommend hiring corps members to other principals.

In order to capture principals' thought processes, both for and against hiring additional corps members, subsequent questions asked all principals to identify the primary reasons they would or would not be inclined to hire corps members in the future, regardless of whether or not they indicated that they would be willing to hire another corps member. Although the vast majority of principals (86 percent) indicated that they would hire additional corps members, almost all of those respondents (93 percent) selected reasons for both hiring and not hiring additional corps members. Of the 14 percent of principals who indicated that they would not hire additional corps members, almost all (95 percent) selected reasons for both hiring and not hiring additional corps members. Because the vast majority of principals identified reasons for both, the following results are reported overall and not disaggregated by whether principals indicated they would or would not hire additional corps members.

As seen in Figure 2.7, classroom management was the only factor that more principals identified as a reason not to hire another corps member (50 percent) than as a reason to hire another corps member (22 percent). Although more than half of principals selected positive experiences with previous corps members and good fit with school culture as reasons they would hire another corps member, more than half also identified the fact that corps members teach for only a two-year commitment as a reason they would not hire another corps member.

Figure 2.7. Reasons Principals Would or Would Not Hire Corps Members

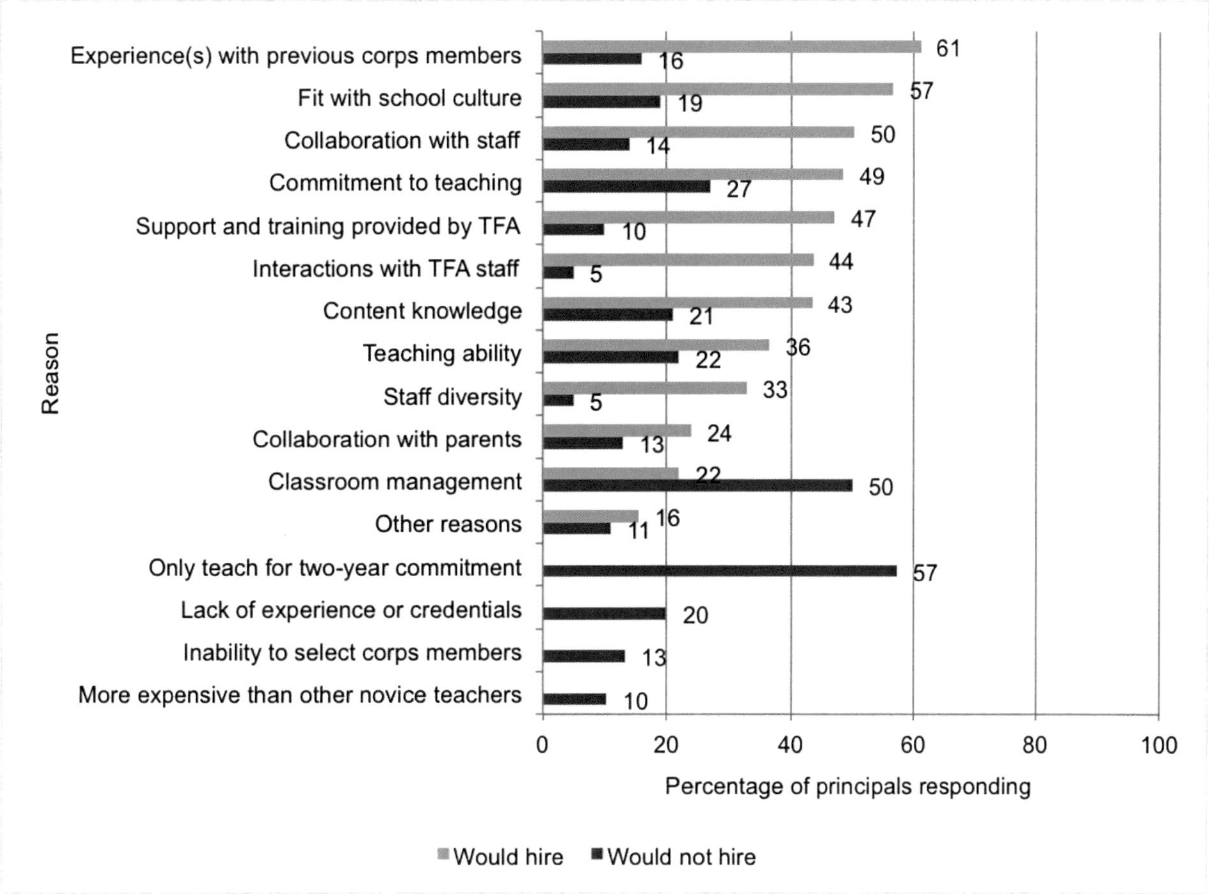

Principal Feedback on Teach For America's Support of Corps Members

Principals Reported Satisfaction with Teach For America's Support of Corps Members

As shown in Figure 2.8, 87 percent of respondents indicated being satisfied with TFA's support of corps members.

Figure 2.8. Principals' Satisfaction with Teach For America's Support of Corps Members

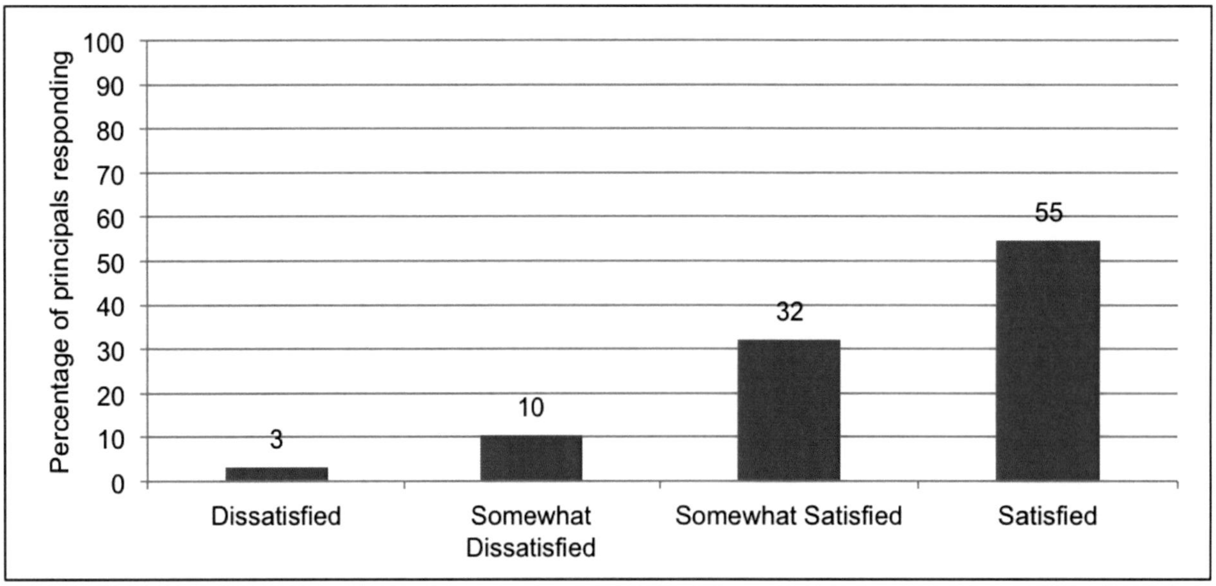

A Majority of Principals Reported That Teach For America's Support Complements School Induction and Training

As shown in Figure 2.9, 78 percent of principals reported that the support that TFA provides corps members complements their schools' induction and training to at least "some extent."

Figure 2.9. Principal's Perceptions of How Well Teach For America's Support Complements Their Schools' Induction and Training

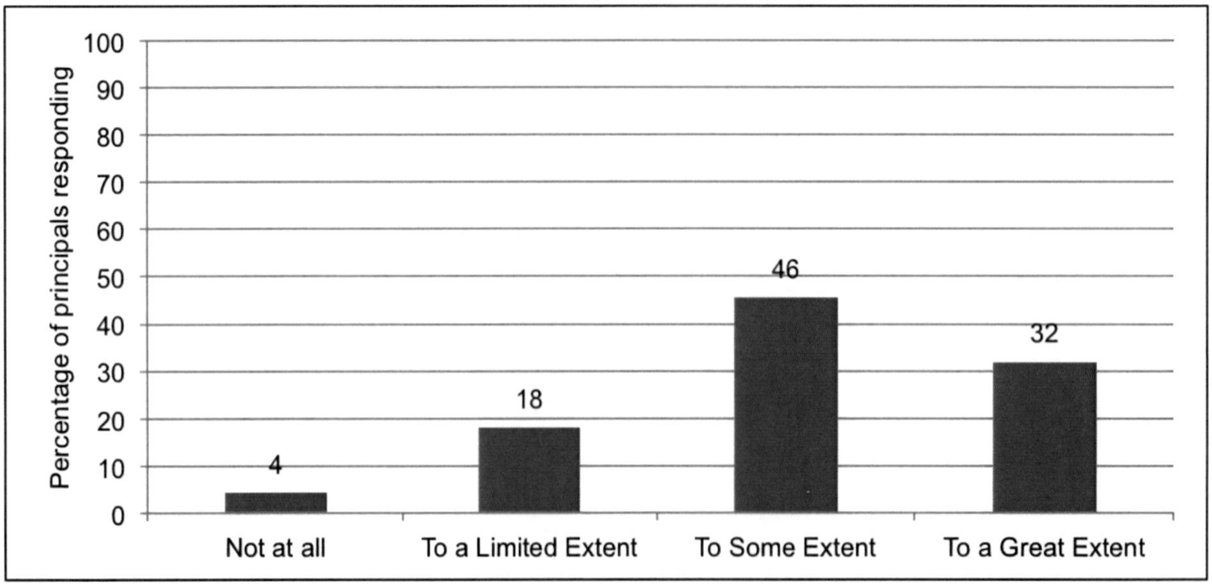

Subgroup Findings

In addition to overall trends, we looked at response differences by the following school and principal characteristics:

- alumni presence at the school
- involvement in the interview process
- principal's alumni status
- school governance structure
- years of experience as a principal
- years of experience as a teacher
- years of principal experience with TFA corps members.

In this section, we highlight overarching trends across groups of respondents and estimates that were statistically significant at the 0.05 level. Because we recorded relevant questions regarding satisfaction with corps members as ordinal variables, we used ordinal logistic regression to test the significance of associations between those variables and the variables listed above. To account for the issue that arises from making multiple comparisons of variables, we adjusted *p*-values from the tests using the false-discovery-rate approach (Benjamini and Hochberg, 1995). Appendix A summarizes the results from the comparisons between the above groups of respondents and survey responses.

There were no significant differences between any of the subgroups we examined and ratings of overall corps members' satisfaction. However, TFA alumni leaders and charter school leaders tended to rate corps members' abilities and the supports that TFA provides lower than principals who were not in those groups. Conversely, principals who had more experience as principals and those who had more experience teaching tended to rate corps members' abilities and the support that TFA provides higher than other principals with less experience. In this section, we report the specific relationships found.

Principal Characteristics Related to Ratings of Corps Members' Abilities

Significant relationships emerged between how principals rated corps members' abilities and principals' charter school status, years of experience as a teacher, and status as a TFA alumnus. Table 2.1 summarizes the significant findings.[2] Overall, TFA alumni and charter school leaders rated corps members' abilities lower in most areas, whereas principals with more experience as principal and those with more experience as teachers rated corps members' abilities higher in most areas.

---

[2] Appendix A shows the coefficients and adjusted *p*-values for all the relationships tested.

Table 2.1. Significant Relationships Between Principals' Characteristics and Ratings of Corps Members' Abilities

Group	Direction of Relationship	Ability
Alumni	Rated corps members lower	• Have an impact on student performance • Have high expectations for all students • Manage classroom culture and student behavior • Know the subject matter • Involve parents or guardians in the education of their children • Relate to students from a variety of cultural, racial, and socioeconomic backgrounds
Charter school leaders	Rated corps members lower	• Develop positive relationships with colleagues and administrators • Have an impact on student performance • Have high expectations for all students • Manage classroom culture and student behavior • Know the subject matter • Involve parents or guardians in the education of their children • Demonstrate leadership among school staff • Relate to students from a variety of cultural, racial, and socioeconomic backgrounds
Principals with more years of experience as a teacher	Rated corps members higher	• Have high expectations for all students • Manage classroom culture and student behavior • Know the subject matter • Involve parents or guardians in the education of their children • Relate to students from a variety of cultural, racial, and socioeconomic backgrounds
Principals with more years of experience as a principal	Rated corps members higher	• Have high expectations for all students • Manage classroom culture and student behavior • Relate to students from a variety of cultural, racial, and socioeconomic backgrounds

NOTE: The exhibit should be read, "Principals identifying as TFA alumni tended to rate corps members' ability related to knowledge of subject matter lower than that of non-alumni."

Some school characteristics and principal characteristics were also significantly related to perceptions of abilities (see Appendix A for details). For example, principals who had an alumnus presence at their schools rated corps members' abilities to have an impact on student performance and demonstrate leadership among school staff as *significantly higher* than other novice teachers. Principals with more experience working with corps members also rated corps members' abilities to affect student performance *significantly higher* than they rated other novice teachers. On the other hand, TFA alumni and principals of charter schools rated corps members' knowledge of subject matter *significantly lower* than they rated other novice teachers.

Ratings of Participation in School Activities Related to Principal Characteristics

Principals who were TFA alumni and led schools with alumni present were *significantly more likely* than other principals to rate corps members' participation in school activities *higher* than other novice teachers. This was significant for all activities except for the relationship between TFA alumni status and corps members serving on school- or district-wide committees or task forces. Additionally, principals of charter schools were *significantly more likely* than other principals to rate corps members' participation as a department lead or chair or a lead curriculum specialist *higher* than other novice teachers, while principals with more years of experience as principals were *more likely* than less-experienced principals to rate corps members' participation in these areas *lower* than other novice teachers.

Willingness to Hire Additional Corps Members Related to Principal Characteristics

Charter school principals were significantly more likely to report that they would hire TFA corps members if they had vacancies in their schools, despite the fact that charter school principals also rated many corps members' abilities significantly lower than non–charter school principals did.

TFA alumni, charter school leaders, and principals with an alumnus presence at their schools were less likely than other principals to identify many reasons they would hire additional corps members (e.g., strong teaching ability, content knowledge, and commitment to teaching). However, they were also more likely to identify a good fit with the school culture as a reason to hire another corps member. More-experienced principals and principals with more teaching experience, on the other hand, were less likely than less-experienced principals to identify any reason to hire another corps member. Table 2.2 summarizes the relationships between the subgroups of principals and reasons they would hire additional corps members.

Table 2.2. Primary Reasons to Hire a Teach For America Corps Member, by Principal Characteristic

Primary Reason to Hire a TFA Corps Member	TFA Alumni	Charter School	Alumnus Presence at School	More Experience with TFA	More-Experienced Principals	More Teaching Experience
Strong classroom management	—	—	—	—	Less likely	—
Strong teaching ability	Less likely	Less likely	Less likely	—	Less likely	—
Strong content knowledge	Less likely	Less likely	Less likely	—	Less likely	Less likely
Good fit with school culture	More likely	More likely	—	—	—	—
High level of collaboration with staff	—	—	—	—	—	—
High level of collaboration with parents	—	—	—	—	—	—
Quality support and training provided by TFA	Less likely	Less likely	Less likely	—	Less likely	Less likely
Positive experience with previous corps members	—	—	More likely	Less likely	—	—
Positive interactions with TFA staff	Less likely	Less likely	—	—	—	—
Add to staff diversity	—	—	—	—	—	—
Strong commitment to teaching	Less likely	Less likely	Less likely	More likely	Less likely	Less likely

NOTE: — = no pattern was found between the two variables, or the relationship between the two variables was not statistically significant at a 0.05 level. The exhibit should be read, "Principals who are TFA alumni are significantly *less likely* than other principals to identify strong teaching ability, strong content knowledge, quality support and training by TFA, positive interactions with TFA staff, and strong commitment to teaching as primary reasons they would hire corps members. Principals who are TFA alumni are significantly *more likely* than other principals to select good fit with school culture as a primary reason they would hire corps members."

Both charter school leaders and TFA alumni were less likely than non–charter school leaders to identify reasons they would not hire another corps member. Table 2.3 summarizes the relationships between the subgroups of principals and reasons they would not hire additional corps members.

Table 2.3. Primary Reasons Not to Hire a Teach For America Corps Member, by Principal Characteristic

Primary Reason Not to Hire a TFA Corps Member	TFA Alumni	Charter School	More Experience with TFA	More-Experienced Principals	More Teaching Experience	Interview TFA Corps Members
Poor classroom management	—	—	—	—	More likely	—
Poor teaching ability	—	More likely	—	—	—	—
Poor content knowledge	—	More likely	—	—	—	—
Poor fit with school culture	—	—	—	—	—	—
Low level of collaboration with staff	—	—	—	Less likely	—	—
Low level of collaboration with parents	—	—	—	—	—	—
Lack of support and training provided by TFA	—	—	More likely	—	—	—
Negative experience with previous corps members	More likely	—	—	—	—	—
Negative interactions with TFA staff	More likely	More likely	—	—	—	—
Detract from staff diversity	—	—	—	—	—	—
Lack of commitment to teaching	—	More likely	—	More likely	—	—
Lack of experience or credentials	—	More likely	—	—	—	—
Teach for only a two-year commitment	—	—	—	—	—	—
More expensive than other novice teachers	More likely	More likely	—	—	—	—
Inability to select corps members	—	—	—	—	—	Less likely

NOTE: — = no pattern was found between the two variables, or the relationship between the two variables was not statistically significant at a 0.05 level. The exhibit should be read, "Principals who have more experience as principals are significantly *less likely* to identify a low level of collaboration with staff as a reason they would not hire corps members and are significantly *more likely* to identify a lack of commitment to teaching as a reason they would not hire corps members."

Satisfaction with Teach For America Support Related to Principal Characteristics

Principals who identified as being alumni, leaders of charter schools, and principals with an alumnus presence at their schools reported significantly lower levels of satisfaction with TFA's support than principals not in those groups reported. However, principals with more experience as teachers and more experience as principals reported significantly higher levels of satisfaction with TFA's support than principals with less experience reported.

As with general satisfaction about TFA's support, principals who identified as being alumni and leaders of charter schools reported that TFA's training was significantly less complementary to their own schools' training and induction. Yet, principals with more experience as teachers and more experience as principals reported TFA's training as being significantly more complementary.

Teach For America Alumni

More than half of survey respondents indicated that TFA alumni are currently working at their schools as teachers, though 6 percent of survey respondents were unsure whether TFA alumni were currently working at their schools. Table 2.4 shows the range in the number of TFA alumni reported to be in the schools.

Table 2.4. Teach For America Alumni Working at Reporting Schools

Alumni	Percentage of Principals Responding (*N* = 952)
1–3	69
4–6	20
7–9	6
10+	6

NOTE: Responses do not add to 100 percent because of rounding.

Principals with alumni working at their schools were asked to indicate how much they agreed with each of three statements. The results of this question (see Figure 2.10) indicate that principals believed that TFA alumni contributed to their schools in a positive way through their promotion of school culture and community and leadership contributions.

Figure 2.10. Satisfaction with Teach For America Alumni Working in Schools

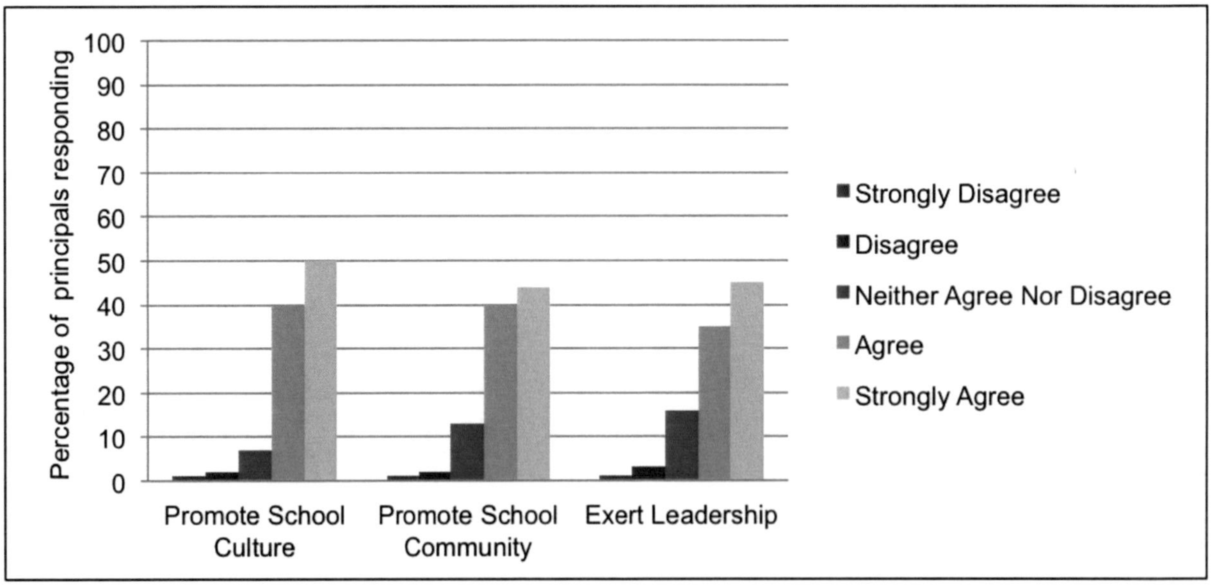

Conclusion

Principals who responded to the 2015 National Principal Survey were generally satisfied with TFA alumni, corps members, and the support TFA provides to corps members. Although principals tended to rate corps members highly in regard to having high expectations for all students and developing relationships with colleagues, they tended to have more-neutral ratings in terms of classroom management and developing relationships with parents.

Generally, charter school principals and principals who were more familiar with TFA (i.e., TFA alumni, principals with TFA alumni working at their school, or more years of experience working with corps members) tended to rate corps members' abilities and the support that TFA provides significantly lower. However, principals with more years of experience as teachers and more years of experience as principals tended to rate corps members' abilities and TFA's support significantly higher. Such findings indicate relationships to explore further and areas that could benefit from additional support from TFA. For example, more information could be sought to understand why charter school leaders and principals who are more familiar with TFA rate corps members' abilities as lower, and TFA could take actions to address such concerns.

Furthermore, most principals were willing to hire additional corps members or recommend hiring corps members to other school leaders. Principals generally identified many more reasons they would hire additional corps members than reasons they would not. Classroom management and the two-year commitment were the only reasons that principals listed more often as reasons to not hire, rather than hire, principals. These findings provide insight into how principals think about hiring corps members. They also identify strengths that TFA should highlight (i.e., reasons principals would hire corps members) when recruiting districts and schools or weaknesses that should be mitigated (i.e., reasons principals would not hire corps members) through additional supports to corps members.

Appendix A: Significance-Test Results

This appendix provides the results of significance testing for all measures and select principal and school characteristics. Table A.1 provides significance-test results for the effect of having interviewed TFA corps members as part of the hiring process and for reporting that their schools employ TFA alumni.

Table A.1. Significance-Test Results for the Effect of a Principal Having Interviewed Corps Members or Heading a School That Employs Teach For America Alumni

	Interview Corps Members			TFA Alumni		
Dependent Variable	**Coefficient**	***p*-Value**	**Adjusted *p*-Value**	**Coefficient**	***p*-Value**	**Adjusted *p*-Value**
Satisfaction with corps members	0.2583	0.0239	0.1971	–0.1073	0.4067	0.5368
Difference made: Academic achievement	0.2656	0.0690	0.3478	0.0635	0.7243	0.8068
Difference made: Socioemotional development	0.1199	0.3858	0.7417	–0.1602	0.3111	0.4431
Difference made: Classroom culture	0.0604	0 .6781	0.8288	–0.2534	0.1193	0.1968
Difference made: School culture and faculty collaboration	0.1989	0.1697	0.4480	–0.1044	0.5400	0.6480
Difference made: Relationships with parents	0.0118	0.9282	0.9572	–0.1027	0.4955	0.6281
Ability: Develop positive relationships with colleagues and administrators	0.0726	0.5276	0.7738	–0.2526	0.0573	0.1112
Ability: Have an impact on student performance	0.1386	0.2270	0.5350	–0.3134	0.0158	0.0387[a]
Ability: Have high expectations for all students	0.0423	0.7148	0.8323	–0.3708	0.0047	0.0134[a]
Ability: Manage classroom culture and student behavior	0.0806	0.4832	0.7417	–0.4182	0.0011	0.0040[a]
Ability: Know the subject matter	0.0844	0.4613	0.7417	–0.8833	0.0000	0.0000[a]
Ability: Involve parents or guardians in the education of their children	–0.0935	0.4125	0.7417	–0.3051	0.0205	0.0467[a]
Ability: Demonstrate leadership among school staff	0.1839	0.1054	0.3478	–0.2580	0.0491	0.1014
Ability: Relate to students from a variety of cultural, racial, and socioeconomic backgrounds	0.1281	0.2598	0.5913	–0.4959	0.0001	0.0006[a]
Novice comparison: Develop positive relationships with colleagues and administrators	0.0494	0.6754	0.8288	–0.1283	0.3470	0.4771
Novice comparison: Have an impact on student performance	0.2064	0.0787	0.3478	0.0008	0.9954	0.9954
Novice comparison: Have high expectations for all students	0.1037	0.3762	0.7417	–0.0047	0.9720	0.9954
Novice comparison: Manage classroom culture and student behavior	0.1443	0.2175	0.5317	0.0852	0.5139	0.6281
Novice comparison: Know the subject matter	–0.0005	0.9963	0.9963	–0.3850	0.0043	0.0131[a]

	Interview Corps Members			TFA Alumni		
Dependent Variable	Coefficient	*p*-Value	Adjusted *p*-Value	Coefficient	*p*-Value	Adjusted *p*-Value
Novice comparison: Involve parents or guardians in the education of their children	−0.0806	0.5069	0.7603	−0.1118	0.4232	0.5477
Novice comparison: Demonstrate leadership among school staff	0.2165	0.0664	0.3478	0.2346	0.0786	0.1400
Novice comparison: Relate to students from a variety of cultural, racial, and socioeconomic backgrounds	0.0567	0.6294	0.8288	−0.1141	0.3881	0.5227
Novice comparison: Coach a sport	0.2184	0.1041	0.3478	0.5962	0.0001	0.0007[a]
Novice comparison: Sponsor any student group, club, or organization	0.1736	0.1817	0.4612	0.4123	0.0059	0.0157[a]
Novice comparison: Serve as a department lead or chair	−0.0756	0.5835	0.8193	0.6354	0.0000	0.0003[a]
Novice comparison: Serve as a lead curriculum specialist	0.0343	0.8098	0.8761	0.6234	0.0002	0.0007[a]
Novice comparison: Serve on a school- or district-wide committee or task force	−0.0339	0.8057	0.8761	0.3253	0.0360	0.0765
Novice comparison: Serve as a formal mentor or mentor coordinator in the school or district	−0.0701	0.6302	0.8288	0.5501	0.0010	0.0039[a]
Would recommend hiring a TFA corps member	0.0990	0.4530	0.7417	−0.2591	0.0806	0.1400
Would hire another corps member	0.2509	0.1454	0.4174	−0.4295	0.0250	0.0550
Satisfaction with TFA support	−0.0287	0.8149	0.8761	−1.0066	0.0000	0.0000[a]
Complementariness of TFA support	0.2087	0.0772	0.3478	−0.8047	0.0000	0.0000[a]
Reason to hire: Strong classroom management	−0.3571	0.0141	0.1777	−0.5695	0.0059	0.0157
Reason to hire: Strong teaching ability	−0.0786	0.5507	0.7901	−0.9059	0.0000	0.0000[a]
Reason to hire: Strong content knowledge	−0.0462	0.7188	0.8323	−0.9645	0.0000	0.0000[a]
Reason to hire: Good fit with school culture	0.2311	0.0709	0.3478	0.8969	0.0000	0.0000[a]
Reason to hire: High level of collaboration with staff	0.0671	0.5990	0.8236	−0.0312	0.8336	0.8733
Reason to hire: High level of collaboration with parents	−0.0333	0.8230	0.8761	−0.2075	0.2533	0.3980
Reason to hire: Quality support and training provided by TFA	−0.2128	0.0957	0.3478	−0.9946	0.0000	0.0000[a]
Reason to hire: Positive experience with previous corps members	0.3636	0.0047	0.1035	0.1550	0.3155	0.4431
Reason to hire: Positive interactions with TFA staff	−0.0462	0.7188	0.8323	−0.6434	0.0001	0.0003[a]
Reason to hire: Add to staff diversity	−0.0995	0.4589	0.7417	−0.1826	0.2598	0.3988
Reason to hire: Strong commitment to teaching	−0.0541	0.6715	0.8288	−0.8021	0.0000	0.0000[a]
Reason to hire: Other	0.1417	0.4362	0.7417	0.8736	0.0000	0.0000[a]
Reasons not to hire: Poor classroom management	−0.0956	0.4651	0.7417	0.2861	0.0630	0.1188
Reasons not to hire: Poor teaching ability	−0.0180	0.9099	0.9532	0.2824	0.1076	0.1821
Reasons not to hire: Poor content knowledge	0.0113	0.9446	0.9591	0.1969	0.2772	0.4158
Reasons not to hire: Poor fit with school culture	−0.0438	0.7921	0.8761	0.0529	0.7842	0.8348

Dependent Variable	Interview Corps Members Coefficient	*p*-Value	Adjusted *p*-Value	TFA Alumni Coefficient	*p*-Value	Adjusted *p*-Value
Reasons not to hire: Low level of collaboration with staff	−0.4747	0.0063	0.1038	−0.2413	0.3127	0.4431
Reasons not to hire: Low level of collaboration with parents	−0.3199	0.0811	0.3478	0.0661	0.7695	0.8326
Reasons not to hire: Lack of support and training provided by TFA	0.1015	0.6525	0.8288	0.1620	0.5058	0.6281
Reasons not to hire: Negative experience with previous corps member	0.3171	0.1006	0.3478	0.5599	0.0024	0.0079[a]
Reasons not to hire: Negative interactions with TFA staff	0.3257	0.3258	0.7090	0.7964	0.0044	0.0131[a]
Reasons not to hire: Detract from staff diversity	1.0095	0.0188	0.1777	0.5478	0.0653	0.1197
Reasons not to hire: Lack of commitment to teaching	0.1060	0.4813	0.7417	0.5241	0.0011	0.0040
Reasons not to hire: Lack of experience or credentials	0.1512	0.3677	0.7417	0.4277	0.0148	0.0375
Reasons not to hire: Teach for only a two-year commitment	−0.1289	0.3330	0.7090	−0.2975	0.0519	0.1039
Reasons not to hire: More expensive than other novice teachers	0.6209	0.0165	0.1777	1.4676	0.0000	0.0000[a]
Reasons not to hire: Inability to select corps members	−0.9117	0.0000	0.0000[a]	0.1140	0.6025	0.7101
Reasons not to hire: Other	0.3187	0.1592	0.4379	0.2811	0.2102	0.3383

NOTE: We report the coefficients for this table in log odds of having a particular characteristic. For example, the log odds that a principal who employs a TFA alumnus rated corps members' abilities to affect student performance is −0.3134, with a *p*-value of 0.0387.
[a] Significant at $p < 0.05$.

Table A.2 provides significance-test results for the effect of working in a charter school and of working in a school with an alumnus present.

Table A.2. Significance-Test Results for Effect of Being from a Charter School or a School That Employs Alumni

Dependent Variable	Charter School Coefficient	*p*-Value	Adjusted *p*-Value	Alumni Presence at School Coefficient	*p*-Value	Adjusted *p*-Value
Satisfaction with corps members	−0.1134	0.2451	0.3370	0.0839	0.3629	0.5323
Difference made: Academic achievement	−0.0407	0.7553	0.8173	0.1050	0.3868	0.5549
Difference made: Socioemotional development	−0.2328	0.0476	0.0897	−0.0707	0.5285	0.6459
Difference made: Classroom culture	−0.3340	0.0060	0.0159	0.1056	0.3623	0.5323
Difference made: School culture and faculty collaboration	−0.0808	0.5254	0.6192	0.1104	0.3507	0.5323

Dependent Variable	Charter School			Alumni Presence at School		
	Coefficient	*p*-Value	Adjusted *p*-Value	Coefficient	*p*-Value	Adjusted *p*-Value
Difference made: Relationships with parents	−0.1972	0.0760	0.1255	−0.2002	0.0553	0.1300
Ability: Develop positive relationships with colleagues and administrators	−0.2702	0.0058	0.0159[a]	−0.0683	0.4580	0.6178
Ability: Have an impact on student performance	−0.2532	0.0091	0.0221[a]	0.0518	0.5696	0.6835
Ability: Have high expectations for all students	−0.3545	0.0003	0.0015[a]	−0.0678	0.4587	0.6178
Ability: Manage classroom culture and student behavior	−0.2616	0.0065	0.0166[a]	−0.0447	0.6212	0.7193
Ability: Know the subject matter	−0.5603	0.0000	0.0000[a]	−0.1223	0.1783	0.3362
Ability: Involve parents or guardians in the education of their children	−0.3489	0.0004	0.0017[a]	−0.0936	0.3028	0.4982
Ability: Demonstrate leadership among school staff	−0.3379	0.0005	0.0021[a]	0.0911	0.3148	0.4982
Ability: Relate to students from a variety of cultural, racial, and socioeconomic backgrounds	−0.3407	0.0004	0.0019[a]	−0.1813	0.0457	0.1160
Novice comparison: Develop positive relationships with colleagues and administrators	−0.1845	0.0672	0.1137	0.1358	0.1477	0.2954
Novice comparison: Have an impact on student performance	−0.0448	0.6513	0.7411	0.2525	0.0064	0.0257[a]
Novice comparison: Have high expectations for all students	−0.1852	0.0620	0.1105	0.2032	0.0283	0.0779
Novice comparison: Manage classroom culture and student behavior	−0.0761	0.4357	0.5228	0.2214	0.0166	0.0521
Novice comparison: Know the subject matter	−0.3610	0.0003	0.0016[a]	−0.0461	0.6186	0.7193
Novice comparison: Involve parents or guardians in the education of their children	−0.2332	0.0257	0.0529	0.1117	0.2469	0.4178
Novice comparison: Demonstrate leadership among school staff	−0.0326	0.7425	0.8167	0.2700	0.0038	0.0177[a]
Novice comparison: Relate to students from a variety of cultural, racial, and socioeconomic backgrounds	−0.1830	0.0654	0.1136	0.0014	0.9876	0.9921
Novice comparison: Coach a sport	0.1284	0.2673	0.3527	0.2689	0.0132	0.0445[a]
Novice comparison: Sponsor any student group, club, or organization	0.0170	0.8789	0.9167	0.2615	0.0125	0.0445[a]
Novice comparison: Serve as a department lead or chair	0.2720	0.0209	0.0444[a]	0.5066	0.0000	0.0000[a]
Novice comparison: Serve as a lead curriculum specialist	0.4048	0.0011	0.0036[a]	0.4726	0.0000	0.0003[a]
Novice comparison: Serve on a school- or district-wide committee or task force	−0.0095	0.9347	0.9347	0.4175	0.0001	0.0009[a]
Novice comparison: Serve as a formal mentor or mentor coordinator in the school or district	0.1529	0.2145	0.3046	0.5544	0.0000	0.0000[a]

Dependent Variable	Charter School Coefficient	Charter School *p*-Value	Charter School Adjusted *p*-Value	Alumni Presence at School Coefficient	Alumni Presence at School *p*-Value	Alumni Presence at School Adjusted *p*-Value
Would recommend hiring a TFA corps member	–0.2734	0.0141	0.0333	0.2067	0.0502	0.1226
Would hire another corps member	–0.3611	0.0152	0.0345[a]	0.0537	0.7059	0.7897
Satisfaction with TFA support	–0.8969	0.0000	0.0000[a]	–0.2753	0.0051	0.0224[a]
Complementariness of TFA support	–0.7437	0.0000	0.0000[a]	–0.1998	0.0337	0.0890
Reason to hire: Strong classroom management	–0.1724	0.2029	0.2976	–0.1431	0.2412	0.4178
Reason to hire: Strong teaching ability	–0.6997	0.0000	0.0000	–0.3398	0.0013	0.0070
Reason to hire: Strong content knowledge	–0.4981	0.0000	0.0001	–0.2783	0.0066	0.0257
Reason to hire: Good fit with school culture	0.5797	0.0000	0.0000	0.0028	0.9785	0.9921
Reason to hire: High level of collaboration with staff	–0.1540	0.1605	0.2407	–0.0043	0.9664	0.9921
Reason to hire: High level of collaboration with parents	–0.2740	0.0401	0.0778	–0.1494	0.2048	0.3654
Reason to hire: Quality support and training provided by TFA	–0.7383	0.0000	0.0000	–0.3256	0.0014	0.0070
Reason to hire: Positive experience with previous corps members	0.0576	0.6096	0.7059	0.6139	0.0000	0.0000
Reason to hire: Positive interactions with TFA staff	–0.5274	0.0000	0.0000	–0.1583	0.1210	0.2577
Reason to hire: Add to staff diversity	–0.1831	0.1231	0.1889	–0.0753	0.4856	0.6392
Reason to hire: Strong commitment to teaching	–0.4246	0.0001	0.0009	–0.3840	0.0002	0.0010
Reason to hire: Other	0.4722	0.0009	0.0031	0.3530	0.0135	0.0445
Reasons not to hire: Poor classroom management	0.1077	0.3353	0.4256	–0.1043	0.3171	0.4982
Reasons not to hire: Poor teaching ability	0.4366	0.0008	0.0027	–0.0437	0.7292	0.7999
Reasons not to hire: Poor content knowledge	0.3822	0.0038	0.0115	0.0013	0.9921	0.9921
Reasons not to hire: Poor fit with school culture	0.0180	0.8994	0.9167	–0.2510	0.0571	0.1300
Reasons not to hire: Low level of collaboration with staff	–0.1922	0.2511	0.3382	–0.3368	0.0250	0.0718
Reasons not to hire: Low level of collaboration with parents	0.0637	0.7002	0.7832	–0.2320	0.1363	0.2810
Reasons not to hire: Lack of support and training provided by TFA	0.3705	0.0363	0.0726	–0.0458	0.7941	0.8454
Reasons not to hire: Negative experience with previous corps member	0.2755	0.0596	0.1093	–0.1089	0.4391	0.6166
Reasons not to hire: Negative interactions with TFA staff	0.6510	0.0055	0.0157	0.0804	0.7393	0.7999
Reasons not to hire: Detract from staff diversity	0.4065	0.0887	0.1428	0.5969	0.0209	0.0628
Reasons not to hire: Lack of commitment to	0.4594	0.0002	0.0010	0.1574	0.1836	0.3366

Dependent Variable	Charter School Coefficient	Charter School p-Value	Charter School Adjusted p-Value	Alumni Presence at School Coefficient	Alumni Presence at School p-Value	Alumni Presence at School Adjusted p-Value
teaching						
Reasons not to hire: Lack of experience or credentials	0.3197	0.0174	0.0383	−0.0829	0.5213	0.6459
Reasons not to hire: Teach for only a two-year commitment	−0.1859	0.0983	0.1545	0.1419	0.1771	0.3362
Reasons not to hire: More expensive than other novice teachers	1.4670	0.0000	0.0000	0.2986	0.0909	0.2000
Reasons not to hire: Inability to select corps members	0.1763	0.2725	0.3527	−0.1043	0.4939	0.6392
Reasons not to hire: Other	0.5525	0.0008	0.0027	−0.1077	0.5093	0.6459

NOTE: We report the coefficients for this table in log odds of having a particular characteristic.
[a] Significant at $p < 0.05$.

Table A.3 provides significance-test results for the effect of principals' experience with TFA corps members and as teachers on different outcomes.

Table A.3. Significance-Test Results for the Effect of Experience with Corps Members and as Teachers

Dependent Variable	Years Experience with Corps Members Coefficient	Years Experience with Corps Members p-Value	Years Experience with Corps Members Adjusted p-Value	Years Experience as a Teacher Coefficient	Years Experience as a Teacher p-Value	Years Experience as a Teacher Adjusted p-Value
Satisfaction with corps members	0.2091	0.0692	0.2404	0.0084	0.3204	0.5422
Difference made: Academic achievement	0.2016	0.1656	0.4554	−0.0010	0.9264	0.9406
Difference made: Socioemotional development	−0.0288	0.8349	0.9180	0.0093	0.3611	0.5812
Difference made: Classroom culture	−0.0137	0.9230	0.9518	0.0194	0.0789	0.2265
Difference made: School culture and faculty collaboration	0.0990	0.4927	0.7390	0.0085	0.4349	0.6378
Difference made: Relationships with parents	−0.0284	0.8259	0.9180	0.0095	0.3108	0.5398
Ability: Develop positive relationships with colleagues and administrators	−0.0267	0.8144	0.9180	0.0181	0.0292	0.1135
Ability: Have an impact on student performance	0.1082	0.3375	0.6020	0.0196	0.0149	0.0655
Ability: Have high expectations for all students	0.0956	0.4019	0.6469	0.0245	0.0029	0.0211[a]
Ability: Manage classroom culture and student behavior	0.0051	0.9640	0.9640	0.0270	0.0008	0.0063[a]

Dependent Variable	Years Experience with Corps Members			Years Experience as a Teacher		
	Coefficient	*p*-Value	Adjusted *p*-Value	Coefficient	*p*-Value	Adjusted *p*-Value
Ability: Know the subject matter	–0.0802	0.4763	0.7311	0.0293	0.0003	0.0042[a]
Ability: Involve parents or guardians in the education of their children	–0.0166	0.8826	0.9253	0.0230	0.0042	0.0254[a]
Ability: Demonstrate leadership among school staff	0.1494	0.1814	0.4741	0.0203	0.0124	0.0621
Ability: Relate to students from a variety of cultural, racial, and socioeconomic backgrounds	0.0164	0.8832	0.9253	0.0319	0.0001	0.0025[a]
Novice comparison: Develop positive relationships with colleagues and administrators	0.1490	0.2033	0.4793	0.0163	0.0499	0.1625
Novice comparison: Have an impact on student performance	0.3744	0.0012	0.0103[a]	0.0071	0.3875	0.6090
Novice comparison: Have high expectations for all students	0.2950	0.0109	0.0657	0.0126	0.1223	0.2958
Novice comparison: Manage classroom culture and student behavior	0.1151	0.3167	0.5980	0.0050	0.5366	0.6965
Novice comparison: Know the subject matter	0.0595	0.6070	0.8149	0.0144	0.0858	0.2277
Novice comparison: Involve parents or guardians in the education of their children	0.1016	0.4010	0.6469	0.0095	0.2724	0.4858
Novice comparison: Demonstrate leadership among school staff	0.3819	0.0010	0.0095	0.0143	0.0862	0.2277
Novice comparison: Relate to students from a variety of cultural, racial, and socioeconomic backgrounds	0.0246	0.8310	0.9180	0.0164	0.0491	0.1625
Novice comparison: Coach a sport	0.3266	0.0143	0.0697	0.0036	0.7113	0.8025
Novice comparison: Sponsor any student group, club, or organization	0.3213	0.0136	0.0697	0.0107	0.2541	0.4658
Novice comparison: Serve as a department lead or chair	0.3092	0.0225	0.0927	–0.0122	0.2054	0.3988
Novice comparison: Serve as a lead curriculum specialist	0.3415	0.0148	0.0697	0.0014	0.8877	0.9155
Novice comparison: Serve on a school- or district-wide committee or task force	0.3198	0.0180	0.0792	0.0147	0.1282	0.2958
Novice comparison: Serve as a formal mentor or mentor coordinator in the school or district	0.2604	0.0652	0.2390	–0.0037	0.7174	0.8025
Would recommend hiring a TFA corps member	0.0417	0.7493	0.8990	0.0218	0.0276	0.1135
Would hire another corps member	0.0993	0.5697	0.7834	–0.0227	0.1047	0.2657
Satisfaction with TFA support	–0.0233	0.8484	0.9180	0.0334	0.0003	0.0042[a]
Complementariness of TFA support	–0.1196	0.3072	0.5980	0.0327	0.0001	0.0025[a]

Dependent Variable	Years Experience with Corps Members			Years Experience as a Teacher		
	Coefficient	*p*-Value	Adjusted *p*-Value	Coefficient	*p*-Value	Adjusted *p*-Value
Reason to hire: Strong classroom management	0.1450	0.3171	0.5980	–0.0098	0.3569	0.5812
Reason to hire: Strong teaching ability	0.1273	0.3285	0.6020	–0.0138	0.1387	0.3051
Reason to hire: Strong content knowledge	0.1455	0.2546	0.5601	–0.0322	0.0005	0.0052[a]
Reason to hire: Good fit with school culture	0.0778	0.5444	0.7674	0.0126	0.1676	0.3457
Reason to hire: High level of collaboration with staff	–0.1126	0.3737	0.6325	0.0117	0.1966	0.3933
Reason to hire: High level of collaboration with parents	0.0438	0.7628	0.8990	–0.0051	0.6266	0.7429
Reason to hire: Quality support and training provided by TFA	–0.0509	0.6881	0.8631	–0.0370	0.0001	0.0025[a]
Reason to hire: Positive experience with previous corps members	–0.9127	0.0000	0.0000[a]	0.0001	0.9877	0.9877
Reason to hire: Positive interactions with TFA staff	–0.0505	0.6931	0.8631	–0.0127	0.1644	0.3457
Reason to hire: Add to staff diversity	0.1242	0.3506	0.6090	–0.0181	0.0546	0.1637
Reason to hire: Strong commitment to teaching	0.3811	0.0027	0.0199[a]	–0.0265	0.0039	0.0254[a]
Reason to hire: Other	–0.1934	0.2930	0.5980	0.0026	0.8331	0.8868
Reasons not to hire: Poor classroom management	–0.0464	0.7222	0.8827	0.0333	0.0005	0.0052[a]
Reasons not to hire: Poor teaching ability	0.2017	0.1981	0.4793	–0.0054	0.6303	0.7429
Reasons not to hire: Poor content knowledge	0.1854	0.2435	0.5541	0.0071	0.5512	0.6965
Reasons not to hire: Poor fit with school culture	0.3550	0.0313	0.1215	0.0272	0.0379	0.1390
Reasons not to hire: Low level of collaboration with staff	0.2399	0.1868	0.4741	0.0043	0.7572	0.8329
Reasons not to hire: Low level of collaboration with parents	0.2063	0.2769	0.5894	0.0119	0.4197	0.6296
Reasons not to hire: Lack of support and training provided by TFA	0.7610	0.0004	0.0047[a]	–0.0039	0.8020	0.8678
Reasons not to hire: Negative experience with previous corps member	–0.0798	0.6634	0.8585	0.0063	0.6298	0.7429
Reasons not to hire: Negative interactions with TFA staff	–0.1812	0.5359	0.7674	0.0145	0.5216	0.6965
Reasons not to hire: Detract from staff diversity	–0.0243	0.9389	0.9533	0.0377	0.1300	0.2958

Dependent Variable	Years Experience with Corps Members Coefficient	p-Value	Adjusted p-Value	Years Experience as a Teacher Coefficient	p-Value	Adjusted p-Value
Reasons not to hire: Lack of commitment to teaching	–0.2196	0.1435	0.4118	0.0283	0.0132	0.0621
Reasons not to hire: Lack of experience or credentials	–0.0805	0.6174	0.8149	0.0049	0.6791	0.7864
Reasons not to hire: Teach for only a two-year commitment	–0.2206	0.0920	0.2892	0.0018	0.8465	0.8868
Reasons not to hire: More expensive than other novice teachers	–0.3309	0.1319	0.3958	0.0207	0.2128	0.4013
Reasons not to hire: Inability to select corps members	0.1488	0.4188	0.6582	0.0101	0.4808	0.6752
Reasons not to hire: Other	0.1264	0.5465	0.7674	–0.0350	0.0087	0.0477

[a] Significant at $p < 0.05$.

Table A.4 reports significance-test results for the effect of an additional year of experience as a principal on different outcomes.

Table A.4. Significance-Test Results for the Effect of Having Experience as a Principal

Dependent Variable	Years Experience as a Principal Coefficient	p-Value	Adjusted p-Value
Satisfaction with corps members	0.0097	0.1938	0.3198
Difference made: Academic achievement	–0.0091	0.3474	0.4525
Difference made: Socioemotional development	0.0084	0.3547	0.4525
Difference made: Classroom culture	0.0036	0.7044	0.7264
Difference made: School culture and faculty collaboration	–0.0047	0.6247	0.6871
Difference made: Relationships with parents	0.0127	0.1347	0.2469
Ability: Develop positive relationships with colleagues and administrators	0.0161	0.0339	0.0973
Ability: Have an impact on student performance	0.0119	0.1074	0.2026
Ability: Have high expectations for all students	0.0194	0.0094	0.0413[a]
Ability: Manage classroom culture and student behavior	0.0139	0.0607	0.1542
Ability: Know the subject matter	0.0255	0.0005	0.0049[a]
Ability: Involve parents or guardians in the education of their children	0.0169	0.0215	0.0678
Ability: Demonstrate leadership among school staff	0.0119	0.1053	0.2026
Ability: Relate to students from a variety of cultural, racial, and socioeconomic backgrounds	0.0254	0.0006	0.0053[a]

	Years Experience as a Principal		
Dependent Variable	Coefficient	*p*-Value	Adjusted *p*-Value
Novice comparison: Develop positive relationships with colleagues and administrators	–0.0034	0.6518	0.6939
Novice comparison: Have an impact on student performance	–0.0092	0.2157	0.3472
Novice comparison: Have high expectations for all students	–0.0098	0.1889	0.3197
Novice comparison: Manage classroom culture and student behavior	0.0006	0.9394	0.9394
Novice comparison: Know the subject matter	0.0133	0.0720	0.1696
Novice comparison: Involve parents or guardians in the education of their children	–0.0083	0.2892	0.4149
Novice comparison: Demonstrate leadership among school staff	–0.0170	0.0249	0.0746
Novice comparison: Relate to students from a variety of cultural, racial, and socioeconomic backgrounds	–0.0061	0.4208	0.5144
Novice comparison: Coach a sport	–0.0198	0.0216	0.0678
Novice comparison: Sponsor any student group, club, or organization	–0.0207	0.0137	0.0534
Novice comparison: Serve as a department lead or chair	–0.0254	0.0037	0.0202[a]
Novice comparison: Serve as a lead curriculum specialist	–0.0239	0.0086	0.0404[a]
Novice comparison: Serve on a school- or district-wide committee or task force	–0.0095	0.2827	0.4146
Novice comparison: Serve as a formal mentor or mentor coordinator in the school or district	–0.0221	0.0159	0.0551
Would recommend hiring a TFA corps member	–0.0094	0.2639	0.4051
Would hire another corps member	0.0187	0.0942	0.1942
Satisfaction with TFA support	0.0306	0.0002	0.0028[a]
Complementariness of TFA support	0.0268	0.0005	0.0049[a]
Reason to hire: Strong classroom management	–0.0373	0.0001	0.0014[a]
Reason to hire: Strong teaching ability	–0.0340	0.0001	0.0014[a]
Reason to hire: Strong content knowledge	–0.0286	0.0005	0.0049[a]
Reason to hire: Good fit with school culture	0.0168	0.0408	0.1076
Reason to hire: High level of collaboration with staff	0.0050	0.5382	0.6124
Reason to hire: High level of collaboration with parents	–0.0171	0.0655	0.1601
Reason to hire: Quality support and training provided by TFA	–0.0218	0.0079	0.0404[a]
Reason to hire: Positive experience with previous corps members	0.0034	0.6815	0.7140
Reason to hire: Positive interactions with TFA staff	–0.0081	0.3238	0.4453
Reason to hire: Add to staff diversity	–0.0044	0.6111	0.6836

Dependent Variable	Years Experience as a Principal		
	Coefficient	*p*-Value	Adjusted *p*-Value
Reason to hire: Strong commitment to teaching	–0.0360	0.0000	0.0010[a]
Reason to hire: Other	0.0363	0.0032	0.0189[a]
Reasons not to hire: Poor classroom management	0.0144	0.0844	0.1857
Reasons not to hire: Poor teaching ability	–0.0115	0.2444	0.3841
Reasons not to hire: Poor content knowledge	0.0223	0.0399	0.1076
Reasons not to hire: Poor fit with school culture	–0.0137	0.1860	0.3197
Reasons not to hire: Low level of collaboration with staff	–0.0337	0.0030	0.0189[a]
Reasons not to hire: Low level of collaboration with parents	–0.0176	0.1428	0.2548
Reasons not to hire: Lack of support and training provided by TFA	–0.0017	0.9014	0.9153
Reasons not to hire: Negative experience with previous corps member	0.0052	0.6489	0.6939
Reasons not to hire: Negative interactions with TFA staff	–0.0158	0.3841	0.4784
Reasons not to hire: Detract from staff diversity	0.0136	0.4963	0.5904
Reasons not to hire: Lack of commitment to teaching	0.0251	0.0111	0.0459[a]
Reasons not to hire: Lack of experience or credentials	–0.0097	0.3417	0.4525
Reasons not to hire: Teach for only a two-year commitment	–0.0210	0.0148	0.0542
Reasons not to hire: More expensive than other novice teachers	0.0260	0.0783	0.1783
Reasons not to hire: Inability to select corps members	–0.0110	0.3565	0.4525
Reasons not to hire: Other	0.0091	0.5010	0.5904

[a] Significant at $p < 0.05$.

Appendix B: 2015 National Principal Survey Instrument Responses

In this appendix, we provide the items on the instrument and the overall results for each item. Note that some percentage sets do not sum to 100 because of rounding.

1. How long have you worked with Teach For America corps members in your capacity as a principal (either in your current school or in a previous role)?

Response	Percentage of Principals (*N* = 1,794)
0–1 year	24
2–3 years	37
4–5 years	22
6+ years	17

2. When responding to the following, please only consider Teach For America corps members that teach in your school during the current (2014–2015) school year. Please tell us whether Teach For America corps members make negative, no, or positive difference in terms of:

	Percentage of Principals Responding (*N* = 1,771)		
Area of Impact	**Negative Difference**	**No Difference**	**Positive Difference**
Academic achievement	4	18	77
Socioemotional development	3	25	71
Classroom culture	7	18	75
School culture and faculty collaboration	5	19	76
Relationships with parents	3	35	62

3. Do you feel Teach For America corps members in your school are poor, fair, good, very good, or excellent in each of the following areas?

	Percentage of Principals Responding (*N* = 1,757)				
Ability	**Poor**	**Fair**	**Good**	**Very Good**	**Excellent**
Developing positive relationships with colleagues and administrators	2	9	25	37	27
Having an impact on student performance	4	15	27	33	21
Having high expectations for all students	3	11	23	34	30
Managing classroom culture and student behavior	9	21	28	25	17
Knowledge of subject matter	3	14	27	33	23
Involving parents and/or guardians in the education of their children	4	23	34	25	14
Demonstrating leadership among school staff	6	21	31	26	15
Relating to students from a variety of cultural, racial, and socioeconomic backgrounds	5	17	27	29	22

4. Compared with other novice teachers (e.g., those with less than 2 years of teaching experience) in your school, would you say Teach For America corps members in your school are much less proficient, somewhat less proficient, the same, somewhat more proficient, or much more proficient at:

	Percentage of Principals Responding (*N* = 1,736)				
Ability	**Much Less Proficient**	**Somewhat Less Proficient**	**The Same**	**Somewhat More Proficient**	**Much More Proficient**
Developing positive relationships with colleagues and administrators	2	8	45	29	15
Having an impact on student performance	3	9	38	35	16
Having high expectations for all students	2	6	38	34	20
Managing classroom culture and student behavior	6	17	40	26	12
Knowledge of subject matter	3	12	41	30	15
Involving parents and/or guardians in the education of their children	2	11	55	23	10
Demonstrating leadership among school staff	3	11	43	28	14
Relating to students from a variety of cultural, racial, and socioeconomic backgrounds	3	11	44	28	14

5. During this school year, to what extent did Teach For America corps members participate in the following?

Activity	No Corps Member	Some Corps Members	All Corps Members	Not Sure
	Percentage of Principals Responding (*N* = 1,733)			
Coach a Sport	60	32	5	3
Sponsor Any Student Groups, Clubs, or Organizations	36	47	15	2
Serve as a Department Lead or Chair	68	27	4	1
Serve as a Lead Curriculum Specialist	81	15	2	1
Serve on a School-Wide or District-Wide Committee or Task Force	44	39	16	1
Serve as a Formal Mentor or Mentor Coordinator in Your School or District	76	20	2	2

6. To what extent did Teach For America corps members participate in the following, compared to other novice teachers?

Activity	Less Than Other Novice Teachers	The Same as Other Novice Teachers	More Than Other Novice Teachers	Not Sure
	Percentage of Principals Responding (*N* = 1,729)			
Coach a Sport	20	60	13	7
Sponsor Any Student Groups, Clubs, or Organizations	17	60	19	4
Serve as a Department Lead or Chair	17	64	13	5
Serve as a Lead Curriculum Specialist	18	66	9	6
Serve on a School-Wide or District-Wide Committee or Task Force	15	64	16	5
Serve as a Formal Mentor or Mentor Coordinator in Your School or District	18	66	8	7

7. To what extent do you agree with the following statement? I am satisfied with the Teach For America corps members in my school.

Response	Percentage of Principals Responding (*N* = 1,732)
Strongly Disagree	9
Moderately Disagree	5
Somewhat Disagree	6
Somewhat Agree	13
Moderately Agree	26
Strongly agree	42

8. Would you recommend hiring a Teach For America corps member to a fellow school leader?

Response	Percentage of Principals Responding (*N* = 1,731)
Definitely Would Not Recommend	4
Unsure/Might or Might Not Recommend	30
Definitely Would Recommend	66

9. If you had a teaching vacancy at your school, would you hire another Teach For America corps member?

Response	Percentage of Principals Responding (*N* = 1,722)
Yes	86
No	14

Regardless of your response to the previous question, the following two questions ask about the reasons you would or would not consider hiring another Teach For America corps member.

10. What are the primary reason(s) you would be willing to hire a Teach For America corps member? (Check all that apply.)

Reason	Percentage of Principals Responding (*N* = 1,713)
Strong Classroom Management	22
Strong Teaching Ability	36
Strong Content Knowledge	43
Good Fit with School Culture	57
High Level of Collaboration with Staff	50
High Level of Collaboration with Parents	24
Quality Support and Training Provided by Teach For America	47
Positive Experience(s) with Previous Corps Members	61
Positive Interactions with Teach For America staff	44
Add to Staff Diversity	33
Strong Commitment to Teaching	49
Other, Please Specify	16

11. What are the primary reason(s) you would not be willing to hire a Teach For America corps member? (Check all that apply.)

Reason	Percentage of Principals Responding (*N* = 1,624)
Poor Classroom Management	50
Poor Teaching Ability	22
Poor Content Knowledge	21
Poor Fit with School Culture	19
Low Level of Collaboration with Staff	14
Low Level of Collaboration with Parents	13
Lack of Support and Training Provided by Teach For America	10
Negative Experience(s) with Previous Corps Members	16
Negative Interactions with Teach For America Staff	5
Detract from Staff Diversity	5
Lack of Commitment to Teaching	27
Lack of Experience or Credentials	20
Only Teach for Two-Year Commitment	57
More Expensive Than Other Novice Teachers	10
Inability to Select Corps Members	13
Other, Please Specify	11

12. Overall, how satisfied are you with the support Teach For America provides corps members in your school?

Response	Percentage of Principals Responding (*N* = 1,724)
Dissatisfied	3
Somewhat Dissatisfied	10
Somewhat Satisfied	32
Satisfied	55

13. To what extent does the support that Teach For America corps members are provided complement your school's induction and training?

Response	Percentage of Principals Responding (*N* = 1,718)
Not at All	4
To a Limited Extent	18
To Some Extent	46
To a Great Extent	32

14. How many full-time equivalent teachers are in your school?

Response	Percentage of Principals Responding (*N* = 1,710)
≤10 teachers	34
11–20 teachers	12
21–30 teachers	16
31–40 teachers	14
41–50 teachers	8
51–60 teachers	6
60+ teachers	10

15. Are teachers at your school given common planning time (e.g., shared time during the school day in which groups of teachers can plan curricula, review data, or participate in professional development)?

Response	Percentage of Principals Responding (*N* = 1,719)
Yes	94
No	6

16. Is your school . . .

	Percentage of Principals Responding	
School Type	Yes	No
A Charter School (*N* = 1,705)	27	73
A Private School (*N* = 1,653)	1	99
An Early Childhood Education Center (*N* = 1,657)	5	95
Managed by the Bureau of Indian Education (*N* = 1,653)	1	99

17. Are any Teach For America alumni currently teaching in your school this current (2014–2015) school year?

Response	Percentage of Principals Responding (*N* = 1,717)
Yes	55
No	39
Unsure	6

18. If there are Teach For America alumni currently teaching in your school, how many are working in your school this school year?

Response	Percentage of Principals Responding (*N* = 951)
1–3 alumni	69
4–6 alumni	20
7–9 alumni	6
10+ alumni	6

19. In the following, please only consider Teach For America alumni who are teaching in your school for the current (2014–2015) school year. To what extent do you agree with the following statements?

	Percentage of Principals Responding (*N* = 933)				
Statement	**Strongly Disagree**	**Disagree**	**Neither Agree nor Disagree**	**Agree**	**Strongly Agree**
Teach For America alumni teachers promote a positive, collaborative, professional culture in the school.	1	2	8	40	50
Teach For America alumni teachers promote strong relationships with the school community (including students and their parents/guardians).	1	2	13	40	44
Teach For America alumni teachers exert significant leadership, formal or informal, in the school.	1	3	16	35	45

20. Are you male or female?

Gender	Percentage of Principals Responding (*N* = 1,709)
Male	37
Female	63

21. Are you of Hispanic or Latino origin?

Response	Percentage of Principals Responding (*N* = 1,699)
Yes	14
No	86

22. What is your race? (Check all that apply.)

Race or Ethnicity	Percentage of Principals Responding (*N* = 1,676)
White	54
Black or African-American	38
Asian	3
Native Hawaiian or Other Pacific Islander	0
American Indian or Alaska Native	2
Other, please specify	7

23. Are you enrolled in a state- or federally-recognized tribe?

Response	Percentage of Principals Responding (*N* = 1,698)
Yes	2
No	98

24. What is your year of birth?

Age Calculated, in Years	Percentage of Principals Responding (*N* = 1,646)
25–30	5
31–40	30
41–50	39
51–60	19
60+	7

25. Are you an alumnus/alumna of Teach For America?

Response	Percentage of Principals Responding (*N* = 1,708)
Yes	12
No	88

26. PRIOR to this school year, how many years did you serve as the principal of this or any other school?

Response	Percentage of Principals Responding (*N* = 1,702)
0–5 years	63
6–10 years	23
11–15 years	10
16–20 years	3
20+ years	2

27. PRIOR to this school year, how many years did you serve as the principal of THIS school?

Response	Percentage of Principals Responding (*N* = 1,697)
None	20
1 year	25
2 years	16
3 years	12
4 years	8
5 years	4
6 years	4
7 years	3
8 years	2
9 years	2
10 years	1
11+ years	4

28. Have you served in any other school administrative role (e.g., assistant principal, vice principal, dean) of this or any other school?

Response	Percentage of Principals Responding (*N* = 1,707)
Yes	**87**
No	**13**

29. Before you became a principal, how many years of elementary or secondary teaching experience did you have?

Response	Percentage of Principals Responding (*N* = 1,702)
0–5 years	27
6–10 years	39
11–15 years	19
16–20 years	9
20+ years	6

30. Before you became a principal, did you have any management experience outside of the field of education?

Response	Percentage of Principals Responding (*N* = 1,702)
Yes	43
No	57

31. On average throughout the school year, what percentage of time do you estimate that you spend on the following tasks in this school? Rough estimates are sufficient. Please write a percentage in each row. Write 0 if none. Responses should add up to 100%.

Internal administrative tasks, including human resource/personnel issues, regulations, reports, school budget

Response	Percentage of Principals Responding (*N* = 1,662)
≤10 percent of principal's time	20
11–20 percent of principal's time	29
21–30 percent of principal's time	27
31–40 percent of principal's time	13
41–50 percent of principal's time	7
50+ percent of principal's time	4

Curriculum and teaching-related tasks, including teaching, lesson preparation, classroom observations, mentoring teachers

Response	Percentage of Principals Responding (*N* = 1,664)
≤10 percent of principal's time	5
11–20 percent of principal's time	13
21–30 percent of principal's time	27
31–40 percent of principal's time	23
41–50 percent of principal's time	19
50+ percent of principal's time	14

Student interactions, including discipline and academic guidance

Response	Percentage of Principals Responding (*N* = 1,661)
≤10 percent of principal's time	23
11–20 percent of principal's time	38
21–30 percent of principal's time	26
31–40 percent of principal's time	7
41–50 percent of principal's time	4
50+ percent of principal's time	1

Parent interactions, including formal and informal interactions

Response	Percentage of Principals Responding (*N* = 1,656)
≤10 percent of principal's time	52
11–20 percent of principal's time	37
21–30 percent of principal's time	10
31–40 percent of principal's time	0
41–50 percent of principal's time	0
50+ percent of principal's time	0

Other

Response	Percentage of Principals Responding (*N* = 1,299)
≤10 percent of principal's time	92
11–20 percent of principal's time	5
21–30 percent of principal's time	2
31–40 percent of principal's time	0
41–50 percent of principal's time	0
50+ percent of principal's time	1

32. How involved are you in making decisions concerning the hiring of new full-time teachers of this school?

Response	Percentage of Principals Responding (*N* = 1,697)
No Involvement	1
Minor Involvement	1
Moderate Involvement	5
Major Involvement	93

33. Do you participate in interviewing Teach For America corps members?

Response	Percentage of Principals Responding (*N* = 1,694)
Yes	82
No	18

Appendix C: 2015 National Principal Survey Instrument Responses, by Alumni Status

In this appendix, we provide the items on the instrument and the results for each item by whether the respondent employs a TFA alumnus. Note that some percentage sets do not sum to 100 because of rounding.

1. How long have you worked with Teach For America corps members in your capacity as a principal (either in your current school or in a previous role)?

	Percentage of Principals	
Response	Alumni (*N* = 207)	Non-Alumni (*N* = 1,501)
0–1 year	19	25
2–3 years	42	36
4–5 years	20	22
6+ years	19	17

2. When responding to the following, please only consider Teach For America corps members that teach in your school during the current (2014–2015) school year. Please tell us whether Teach For America corps members make negative, no, or positive difference in terms of:

	Percentage of Principals Responding (*N* = 1,772)					
	Negative Difference		No Difference		Positive Difference	
Area of Impact	Alumni (*N* = 207)	Non-Alumni (*N* = ~1,500)	Alumni (*N* = 207)	Non-Alumni (*N* = ~1,500)	Alumni (*N* = 207)	Non-Alumni (*N* = ~1,500)
Academic Achievement	4	5	18	17	79	78
Classroom Culture	8	7	21	17	71	76
Relationship with Parents	2	3	37	34	61	63
School Culture and Faculty Collaboration	3	4	22	19	75	77
Socioemotional Development	2	4	29	24	68	72

3. Do you feel Teach For America corps members in your school are poor, fair, good, very good, or excellent in each of the following areas?

	Percentage of Principals Responding									
	Poor		Fair		Good		Very Good		Excellent	
Ability	**Alumni (*N* = 207)**	**Non-Alumni (*N* = ~1,499)**	**Alumni (*N* = 207)**	**Non-Alumni (*N* = ~1,499)**	**Alumni (*N* = 207)**	**Non-Alumni (*N* = ~1,499)**	**Alumni (*N* = 207)**	**Non-Alumni (*N* = ~1,499)**	**Alumni (*N* = 207)**	**Non-Alumni (*N* = ~1,499)**
Demonstrating Leadership Among School Staff	5	6	26	21	32	31	25	26	11	16
Developing Positive Relationships with Colleagues and Administrators	0	2	11	9	29	24	37	37	22	28
Having an Impact on Student Performance	1	4	18	14	34	26	31	34	15	23
Having High Expectations for All Students	1	3	13	10	30	21	33	34	22	31
Involving Parents and/or Guardians in the Education of Their Children	2	4	29	22	40	34	19	26	11	14
Knowledge of Subject Matter	5	3	27	12	30	26	26	35	13	25
Managing Classroom Culture and Student Behavior	5	9	33	19	31	28	21	26	10	18
Relating to Students From a Variety of Cultural, Racial, and Socioeconomic Backgrounds	3	5	25	16	32	25	28	30	13	24

4. Compared with other novice teachers (e.g., those with less than 2 years of teaching experience) in your school, would you say Teach For America corps members in your school are much less proficient, somewhat less proficient, the same, somewhat more proficient, or much more proficient at:

	Percentage of Principals Responding									
	Much Less Proficient		Somewhat Less Proficient		The Same		Somewhat More Proficient		Much More Proficient	
Ability	**Alumni (*N* = 207)**	**Non-Alumni (*N* = ~1,497)**	**Alumni (*N* = 207)**	**Non-Alumni (*N* = ~1,497)**	**Alumni (*N* = 207)**	**Non-Alumni (*N* = ~1,497)**	**Alumni (*N* = 207)**	**Non-Alumni (*N* = ~1,497)**	**Alumni (*N* = 207)**	**Non-Alumni (*N* = ~1,497)**
Demonstrating Leadership Among School Staff	0	3	9	12	44	43	32	28	15	14
Developing Positive Relationships with Colleagues and Administrators	1	2	8	8	51	44	26	29	14	16
Having an Impact on Student Performance	2	3	9	8	37	37	38	34	14	17
Having High Expectations for All Students	1	2	5	6	40	38	34	34	20	21
Involving Parents and/or Guardians in the Education of Their Children	1	2	9	11	62	53	20	23	8	10
Knowledge of Subject Matter	1	3	16	11	47	40	25	31	10	16
Managing Classroom Culture and Student Behavior	3	6	12	17	47	39	29	25	9	13
Relating to Students From a Variety of Cultural, Racial, and Socioeconomic Backgrounds	1	3	7	11	55	42	27	29	10	15

5. During this school year, to what extent did Teach For America corps members participate in the following?

	Percentage of Principals Responding							
	No Corps Member		Some Corps Members		All Corps Members		Not Sure	
Activity	**Alumni (*N* = 207)**	**Non-Alumni (*N* = ~1,497)**	**Alumni (*N* = 207)**	**Non-Alumni (*N* = ~1,497)**	**Alumni (*N* = 207)**	**Non-Alumni (*N* = ~1,497)**	**Alumni (*N* = 207)**	**Non-Alumni (*N* = ~1,497)**
Coach a Sport	59	61	37	32	3	5	1	3
Serve as a Department Lead or Chair	70	68	27	27	4	4	0	1
Serve as a Formal Mentor or Mentor Coordinator in Your School or District	84	75	14	20	1	3	0	2
Serve as a Lead Curriculum Specialist	82	81	17	15	1	3	0	1
Serve on a School-Wide or District-Wide Committee or Task Force	55	43	34	40	11	16	0	1
Sponsor Any Student Groups, Clubs, or Organizations	37	36	48	47	15	15	0	2

6. To what extent did Teach For America corps members participate in the following, compared to other novice teachers?

	Percentage of Principals Responding							
	Less Than Other Novice Teachers		The Same as Other Novice Teachers		More Than Other Novice Teachers		Not Sure	
Activity	**Alumni (*N* = 207)**	**Non-Alumni (*N* = ~1,496)**	**Alumni (*N* = 207)**	**Non-Alumni (*N* = ~1,496)**	**Alumni (*N* = 207)**	**Non-Alumni (*N* = ~1,496)**	**Alumni (*N* = 207)**	**Non-Alumni (*N* = ~1,496)**
Coach a Sport	12	21	65	60	19	12	5	7
Serve as a Department Lead or Chair	5	19	76	63	16	13	3	5
Serve as a Formal Mentor or Mentor Coordinator in Your School or District	7	20	80	64	7	8	6	7
Serve as a Lead Curriculum Specialist	6	20	81	64	9	9	4	7
Serve on a School-Wide or District-Wide Committee or Task Force	7	16	73	63	16	16	4	5
Sponsor Any Student Groups, Clubs, or Organizations	10	17	63	60	24	19	3	4

7. To what extent do you agree with the following statement? I am satisfied with the Teach For America corps members in my school.

	Percentage of Principals Responding	
Response	**Alumni (*N* = 207)**	**Non-Alumni (*N* = 1,501)**
Strongly Agree	34	43
Moderately Agree	36	25
Somewhat Agree	13	12
Somewhat Disagree	8	5
Moderately Disagree	4	5
Strongly Disagree	5	9

8. Would you recommend hiring a Teach For America corps member to a fellow school leader?

	Percentage of Principals Responding	
Response	**Alumni (*N* = 207)**	**Non-Alumni (*N* = 1,501)**
Definitely Would Recommend	59	67
Unsure/Might or Might Not Recommend	39	29
Definitely Would Not Recommend	1	4

9. If you had a teaching vacancy at your school, would you hire another Teach For America corps member?

	Percentage of Principals Responding	
Response	**Alumni (*N* = 205)**	**Non-Alumni (*N* = 1,497)**
Yes	80	86
No	20	14

Regardless of your response to the previous question, the following two questions ask about the reasons you would or would not consider hiring another Teach For America corps member.

10. What are the primary reason(s) you would be willing to hire a Teach For America corps member? (Check all that apply.)

	Percentage of Principals Responding	
Reason	**Alumni (*N* = 207)**	**Non-Alumni (*N* = 1,488)**
Strong Classroom Management	14	23
Strong Teaching Ability	20	39
Strong Content Knowledge	25	46
Good Fit with School Culture	74	54
High Level of Collaboration with Staff	50	51
High Level of Collaboration with Parents	21	24
Quality Support and Training Provided by Teach For America	27	50
Positive Experience(s) with Previous Corps Members	64	61
Positive Interactions with Teach For America Staff	30	45
Add to Staff Diversity	29	33
Strong Commitment to Teaching	32	51
Other, Please Specify	28	14

NOTE: Calculations assume that all blanks for the question reflect a disagreement with the statement provided. The exhibit should be read, "Of the alumni who responded to this question, 14 percent consider 'strong classroom management' to be a primary reason that they would be willing to hire a Teach For America corps member."

11. What are the primary reason(s) you would not be willing to hire a Teach For America corps member? (Check all that apply.)

	Percentage of Principals Responding	
Reason	**Alumni (*N* = 195)**	**Non-Alumni (*N* = 1,414)**
Poor Classroom Management	56	49
Poor Teaching Ability	26	21
Poor Content Knowledge	24	20
Poor Fit with School Culture	19	19
Low Level of Collaboration with Staff	11	14
Low Level of Collaboration with Parents	13	13
Lack of Support and Training Provided by Teach For America	11	10
Negative Experience(s) with Previous Corps Members	24	15
Negative Interactions with Teach For America Staff	9	4
Detract from Staff Diversity	8	5
Lack of Commitment to Teaching	36	25
Lack of Experience or Credentials	27	19
Only Teach for Two-Year Commitment	51	58
More Expensive than Other Novice Teachers	27	8
Inability to Select Corps Members	14	13
Other, Please Specify	14	11

NOTE: Calculations assume that all blanks for the question reflect a disagreement with the statement provided. The exhibit should be read, "Of the alumni who responded to this question, 56 percent consider 'poor classroom management' to be a primary reason that they would not be willing to hire a Teach For America corps member."

12. Overall, how satisfied are you with the support Teach For America provides corps members in your school?

	Percentage of Principals Responding	
Response	**Alumni (*N* = 207)**	**Non-Alumni (*N* = 1,501)**
Satisfied	34	58
Somewhat Satisfied	39	31
Somewhat Dissatisfied	21	9
Dissatisfied	6	2

13. To what extent does the support that Teach For America corps members are provided complement your school's induction and training?

	Percentage of Principals Responding	
Response	Alumni (*N* = 207)	Non-Alumni (*N* = 1,498)
To a Great Extent	18	34
To Some Extent	44	46
To a Limited Extent	33	16
Not at All	5	4

14. How many full-time equivalent teachers are in your school?

	Percentage of Principals Responding	
Response	Alumni (*N* = 207)	Non-Alumni (*N* = 1,491)
≤10 teachers	17	37
11–20 teachers	24	10
21–30 teachers	24	15
31–40 teachers	18	13
41–50 teachers	8	8
51–60 teachers	4	6
60+ teachers	5	10

15. Are teachers at your school given common planning time (e.g., shared time during the school day in which groups of teachers can plan curricula, review data, or participate in professional development)?

	Percentage of Principals Responding	
Response	Alumni (*N* = 207)	Non-Alumni (*N* = 1,501)
Yes	94	94
No	6	6

16. Is your school . . .

	Percentage of Principals Responding			
	Yes		No	
School Type	Alumni (*N* = ~204)	Non-Alumni (*N* = ~1,453)	Alumni (*N* = ~204)	Non-Alumni (*N* = ~1,453)
A Charter School	75	20	25	80
A Private School	2	1	98	99
An Early Childhood Education Center	2	5	98	95
Managed by the Bureau of Indian Education	0	1	100	99

17. Are any Teach For America alumni currently teaching in your school this current (2014–2015) school year?

	Percentage of Principals Responding	
Response	**Alumni (*N* = 207)**	**Non-Alumni (*N* = 1,501)**
Yes	85	50
No	15	43
Unsure	0	7

18. If there are Teach For America alumni currently teaching in your school, how many are working in your school this school year?

	Percentage of Principals Responding	
Response	**Alumni (*N* = 178)**	**Non-Alumni (*N* = 768)**
1–3 alumni	34	77
4–6 alumni	30	17
7–9 alumni	15	4
10+ alumni	20	2

19. In the following, please only consider Teach For America alumni who are teaching in your school for the current (2014–2015) school year. To what extent do you agree with the following statements?

	Percentage of Principals Responding									
	Strongly Disagree		Disagree		Neither Agree nor Disagree		Agree		Strongly Agree	
Statement	**Alumni (N = 176)**	**Non-Alumni (N = ~752)**	**Alumni (N = 176)**	**Non-Alumni (N = ~752)**	**Alumni (N = 176)**	**Non-Alumni (N = ~752)**	**Alumni (N = 176)**	**Non-Alumni (N = ~752)**	**Alumni (N = 176)**	**Non-Alumni (N = ~752)**
Teach For America alumni teachers promote a positive, collaborative, professional culture in the school.	1	1	1	2	4	8	27	42	68	46
Teach For America alumni teachers promote strong relationships with the school community (including students and their parents/guardians).	1	1	1	2	7	14	30	43	61	40
Teach For America alumni teachers exert significant leadership, formal or informal, in the school.	1	1	2	3	6	18	21	38	70	39

20. Are you male or female?

Gender	Percentage of Principals Responding	
	Alumni (*N* = 207)	Non-Alumni (*N* = 1,495)
Female	62	63
Male	38	37

21. Are you of Hispanic or Latino origin?

Response	Percentage of Principals Responding	
	Alumni (*N* = 207)	Non-Alumni (*N* = 1,495)
Yes	12	15
No	88	85

22. What is your race? (Check all that apply.)

Race or Ethnicity	Percentage of Principals Responding	
	Alumni (*N* = 204)	Non-Alumni (*N* = 1,470)
White	72	51
Black or African-American	20	40
Asian	4	3
Native Hawaiian or Other Pacific Islander	0	1
American Indian or Alaska Native	1	2
Other	8	7

NOTE: Calculations assume that all blanks for the question reflect a disagreement with the statement provided. The exhibit should be read, "Of the alumni who responded to this question, 72 percent identify as being as being white.

23. Are you enrolled in a state- or federally-recognized tribe?

Response	Percentage of Principals Responding	
	Alumni (*N* = 207)	Non-Alumni (*N* = 1,490)
Yes	0	2
No	100	98

24. What is your year of birth?

Age Calculated, in Years	Percentage of Principals Responding	
	Alumni (*N* = 206)	Non-Alumni (*N* = 1,439)
25–30	30	1
31–40	59	26
41–50	11	44
51–60	0	22
60+	0	8

25. Are you an alumnus/alumna of Teach For America?

	Percentage of Principals Responding	
Response	**Alumni (*N* = 207)**	**Non-Alumni (*N* = 1,501)**
Yes	100	0
No	0	100

26. PRIOR to this school year, how many years did you serve as the principal of this or any other school?

	Percentage of Principals Responding	
Response	**Alumni (*N* = 207)**	**Non-Alumni (*N* = 1,491)**
0–5 years	91	59
6–10 years	9	24
11–15 years	0	11
16–20 years	0	3
20+ years	0	2

27. PRIOR to this school year, how many years did you serve as the principal of THIS school?

	Percentage of Principals Responding	
Response	**Alumni (*N* = 207)**	**Non-Alumni (*N* = 1,488)**
None	30	18
1 year	25	25
2 years	16	16
3 years	12	11
4 years	9	8
5 years	3	4
6 years	1	4
7 years	1	3
8 years	0	3
9 years	1	2
10 years	0	2
11+ years	0	4

28. Have you served in any other school administrative role (e.g., assistant principal, vice principal, dean) of this or any other school?

	Percentage of Principals Responding	
Response	**Alumni (*N* = 207)**	**Non-Alumni (*N* = 1,496)**
Yes	75	89
No	25	11

29. Before you became a principal, how many years of elementary or secondary teaching experience did you have?

Response	Percentage of Principals Responding	
	Alumni (*N* = 206)	Non-Alumni (*N* = 1,493)
0–5 years	62	22
6–10 years	33	40
11–15 years	4	21
16–20 years	0	11
20+ years	0	6

30. Before you became a principal, did you have any management experience outside of the field of education?

Response	Percentage of Principals Responding	
	Alumni (*N* = 206)	Non-Alumni (*N* = 1,493)
Yes	30	44
No	70	56

31. On average throughout the school year, what percentage of time do you estimate that you spend on the following tasks in this school? Rough estimates are sufficient. Please write a percentage in each row. Write 0 if none. Responses should add up to 100%.

Internal administrative tasks, including human resource/personnel issues, regulations, reports, school budget

Response	Percentage of Principals Responding	
	Alumni (*N* = 204)	Non-Alumni (*N* = 1,455)
≤10 percent of principal's time	28	18
11–20 percent of principal's time	30	29
21–30 percent of principal's time	25	27
31–40 percent of principal's time	11	13
41–50 percent of principal's time	2	7
50+ percent of principal's time	3	4

Curriculum and teaching-related tasks, including teaching, lesson preparation, classroom observations, mentoring teachers

	Percentage of Principals Responding	
Response	**Alumni (*N* = 204)**	**Non-Alumni (*N* = 1,457)**
≤10 percent of principal's time	5	5
11–20 percent of principal's time	8	14
21–30 percent of principal's time	20	28
31–40 percent of principal's time	30	22
41–50 percent of principal's time	18	19
50+ percent of principal's time	19	13

Student interactions, including discipline and academic guidance

	Percentage of Principals Responding	
Response	**Alumni (*N* = 204)**	**Non-Alumni (*N* = 1,454)**
≤10 percent of principal's time	16	24
11–20 percent of principal's time	42	38
21–30 percent of principal's time	32	26
31–40 percent of principal's time	8	7
41–50 percent of principal's time	2	4
50+ percent of principal's time	0	1

Parent interactions, including formal and informal interactions

	Percentage of Principals Responding	
Response	**Alumni (*N* = 204)**	**Non-Alumni (*N* = 1,449)**
≤10 percent of principal's time	56	52
11–20 percent of principal's time	36	37
21–30 percent of principal's time	7	10
31–40 percent of principal's time	0	1
41–50 percent of principal's time	0	0
50+ percent of principal's time	0	1

Other

Response	Percentage of Principals Responding	
	Alumni (*N* = 204)	Non-Alumni (*N* = 1,457)
≤10 percent of principal's time	88	93
11–20 percent of principal's time	9	4
21–30 percent of principal's time	2	2
31–40 percent of principal's time	1	0
41–50 percent of principal's time	1	0
50+ percent of principal's time	0	1

32. How involved are you in making decisions concerning the hiring of new full-time teachers of this school?

Response	Percentage of Principals Responding	
	Alumni (*N* = 205)	Non-Alumni (*N* = 1,488)
No Involvement	0	1
Minor Involvement	0	1
Moderate Involvement	1	5
Major Involvement	99	93

33. Do you participate in interviewing Teach For America corps members?

Response	Percentage of Principals Responding	
	Alumni (*N* = 205)	Non-Alumni (*N* = 1,486)
Yes	89	81
No	11	19

Appendix D: 2015 National Principal Survey Instrument Responses, by Charter Status

In this appendix, we provide the items on the instrument and the results for each item by whether the respondent's school is charter school. Note that some percentage sets do not sum to 100 because of rounding.

1. How long have you worked with Teach For America corps members in your capacity as a principal (either in your current school or in a previous role)?

	Percentage of Principals	
Response	**Charter (*N* = 460)**	**Non-Charter (*N* = 1,245)**
0–1 year	22	25
2–3 years	39	36
4–5 years	23	21
6+ years	17	17

2. When responding to the following, please only consider Teach For America corps members that teach in your school during the current (2014–2015) school year. Please tell us whether Teach For America corps members make negative, no, or positive difference in terms of:

	Percentage of Principals Responding (*N* = 1,772)					
	Negative Difference		No Difference		Positive Difference	
Area of Impact	**Charter (*N* = 460)**	**Non-Charter (*N* = ~1,244)**	**Charter (*N* = 460)**	**Non-Charter (*N* = ~1,244)**	**Charter (*N* = 460)**	**Non-Charter (*N* = ~1,244)**
Academic Achievement	5	4	18	17	78	78
Classroom Culture	9	6	20	17	71	77
Relationship with Parents	3	2	37	33	60	64
School Culture and Faculty Collaboration	4	4	20	18	76	77
Socioemotional Development	3	3	28	24	68	73

3. Do you feel Teach For America corps members in your school are poor, fair, good, very good, or excellent in each of the following areas?

	Percentage of Principals Responding									
	Poor		Fair		Good		Very Good		Excellent	
Ability	Charter (N = 460)	Non-Charter (N = ~1,243)	Charter (N = 460)	Non-Charter (N = ~1,243)	Charter (N = 460)	Non-Charter (N = ~1,243)	Charter (N = 460)	Non-Charter (N = ~1,243)	Charter (N = 460)	Non-Charter (N = ~1,243)
Demonstrating Leadership Among School Staff	6	6	25	20	34	30	24	27	11	17
Developing Positive Relationships with Colleagues and Administrators	1	2	10	9	29	23	39	37	22	30
Having an Impact on Student Performance	2	4	17	14	30	26	34	33	17	23
Having High Expectations for All Students	2	3	13	10	27	21	35	34	23	33
Involving Parents and/or Guardians in the Education of Their Children	3	4	27	21	38	33	21	27	11	15
Knowledge of Subject Matter	4	2	19	12	30	25	31	34	16	26
Managing Classroom Culture and Student Behavior	8	9	24	20	32	27	23	26	13	19
Relating to Students From a Variety of Cultural, Racial, and Socioeconomic Backgrounds	4	5	20	16	31	25	29	30	16	25

4. Compared with other novice teachers (e.g., those with less than 2 years of teaching experience) in your school, would you say Teach For America corps members in your school are much less proficient, somewhat less proficient, the same, somewhat more proficient, or much more proficient at:

	Percentage of Principals Responding									
	Much Less Proficient		Somewhat Less Proficient		The Same		Somewhat More Proficient		Much More Proficient	
Ability	**Charter (*N* = ~458)**	**Non-Charter (*N* = ~1,242)**	**Charter (*N* = ~458)**	**Non-Charter (*N* = ~1,242)**	**Charter (*N* = ~458)**	**Non-Charter (*N* = ~1,242)**	**Charter (*N* = ~458)**	**Non-Charter (*N* = ~1,242)**	**Charter (*N* = ~458)**	**Non-Charter (*N* = ~1,242)**
Demonstrating Leadership Among School Staff	3	3	9	12	47	42	29	28	12	15
Developing Positive Relationships with Colleagues and Administrators	2	2	7	9	53	43	25	30	14	16
Having an Impact on Student Performance	2	3	9	9	40	37	36	34	14	17
Having High Expectations for All Students	1	2	5	6	43	37	35	33	16	22
Involving Parents and/or Guardians in the Education of Their Children	2	2	12	10	58	53	20	23	8	11
Knowledge of Subject Matter	3	3	15	10	45	40	27	31	11	16
Managing Classroom Culture and Student Behavior	5	6	14	17	47	38	24	26	9	13
Relating to Students From a Variety of Cultural, Racial, and Socioeconomic Backgrounds	1	3	10	11	51	41	26	29	11	15

5. During this school year, to what extent did Teach For America corps members participate in the following?

	Percentage of Principals Responding							
	No Corps Member		Some Corps Members		All Corps Members		Not Sure	
Activity	**Charter (*N* = ~459)**	**Non-Charter (*N* = ~1,243)**	**Charter (*N* = ~459)**	**Non-Charter (*N* = ~1,243)**	**Charter (*N* = ~459)**	**Non-Charter (*N* = ~1,243)**	**Charter (*N* = ~459)**	**Non-Charter (*N* = ~1,243)**
Coach a Sport	63	60	33	32	3	5	1	3
Serve as a Department Lead or Chair	69	68	28	26	3	4	0	1
Serve as a Formal Mentor or Mentor Coordinator in Your School or District	79	75	18	20	2	2	0	2
Serve as a Lead Curriculum Specialist	81	81	17	15	2	2	0	2
Serve on a School-Wide or District-Wide Committee or Task Force	51	42	37	40	12	17	0	1
Sponsor Any Student Groups, Clubs, or Organizations	35	36	51	46	13	16	1	2

6. To what extent did Teach For America corps members participate in the following, compared to other novice teachers?

	Percentage of Principals Responding							
	Less Than Other Novice Teachers		The Same as Other Novice Teachers		More Than Other Novice Teachers		Not Sure	
Activity	Charter (N = ~460)	Non-Charter (N = ~1,240)	Charter (N = ~460)	Non-Charter (N = ~1,240)	Charter (N = ~460)	Non-Charter (N = ~1,240)	Charter (N = ~460)	Non-Charter (N = ~1,240)
Coach a Sport	18	20	63	60	13	12	6	7
Serve as a Department Lead or Chair	13	19	69	63	13	13	5	5
Serve as a Formal Mentor or Mentor Coordinator in Your School or District	15	20	71	65	7	9	6	7
Serve as a Lead Curriculum Specialist	13	20	72	64	10	8	6	7
Serve on a School-Wide or District-Wide Committee or Task Force	12	17	71	62	12	17	5	5
Sponsor Any Student Groups, Clubs, or Organizations	15	17	64	59	18	20	3	4

7. To what extent do you agree with the following statement? I am satisfied with the Teach For America corps members in my school.

	Percentage of Principals Responding	
Response	**Charter (*N* = 460)**	**Non-Charter (*N* = 1,245)**
Strongly Agree	37	43
Moderately Agree	32	24
Somewhat Agree	13	13
Somewhat Disagree	5	6
Moderately Disagree	5	5
Strongly Disagree	7	9

8. Would you recommend hiring a Teach For America corps member to a fellow school leader?

	Percentage of Principals Responding	
Response	**Charter (*N* = 460)**	**Non-Charter (*N* = 1,245)**
Definitely Would Recommend	61	68
Unsure/Might or Might Not Recommend	36	28
Definitely Would Not Recommend	3	4

9. If you had a teaching vacancy at your school, would you hire another Teach For America corps member?

	Percentage of Principals Responding	
Response	**Charter (*N* = 457)**	**Non-Charter (*N* = 1,241)**
Yes	82	87
No	18	13

Regardless of your response to the previous question, the following two questions ask about the reasons you would or would not consider hiring another Teach For America corps member.

10. What are the primary reason(s) you would be willing to hire a Teach For America corps member? (Check all that apply.)

	Percentage of Principals Responding	
Reason	**Charter (*N* = 456)**	**Non-Charter (*N* = 1,234)**
Strong Classroom Management	20	23
Strong Teaching Ability	25	40
Strong Content Knowledge	35	47
Good Fit with School Culture	67	53
High Level of Collaboration with Staff	47	51
High Level of Collaboration with Parents	20	25
Quality Support and Training Provided by Teach For America	34	52
Positive Experience(s) with Previous Corps Members	62	61
Positive Interactions with Teach For America Staff	34	47
Add to Staff Diversity	30	34
Strong Commitment to Teaching	41	51
Other, Please Specify	20	14

NOTE: Calculations assume that all blanks for the question reflect a disagreement with the statement provided. The exhibit should be read, "Of the principals leading charter schools who responded to this question, 20 percent consider 'strong classroom management' to be a primary reason that they would be willing to hire a Teach For America corps member."

11. What are the primary reason(s) you would not be willing to hire a Teach For America corps member? (Check all that apply.)

	Percentage of Principals Responding	
Reason	**Charter (*N* = 442)**	**Non-Charter (*N* = 1,164)**
Poor Classroom Management	52	50
Poor Teaching Ability	27	20
Poor Content Knowledge	26	19
Poor Fit with School Culture	19	19
Low Level of Collaboration with Staff	12	14
Low Level of Collaboration with Parents	13	13
Lack of Support and Training Provided by Teach For America	12	9
Negative Experience(s) with Previous Corps Members	19	15
Negative Interactions with Teach For America Staff	7	4
Detract from Staff Diversity	7	4
Lack of Commitment to Teaching	34	24
Lack of Experience or Credentials	24	19
Only Teach for Two-Year Commitment	54	58
More Expensive than Other Novice Teachers	22	6
Inability to Select Corps Members	15	13
Other, Please Specify	16	10

NOTE: Calculations assume that all blanks for the question reflect a disagreement with the statement provided. The exhibit should be read, "Of the principals leading charter schools who responded to this question, 52 percent consider 'poor classroom management' to be a primary reason that they would not be willing to hire a Teach For America corps member."

12. Overall, how satisfied are you with the support Teach For America provides corps members in your school?

	Percentage of Principals Responding	
Response	**Charter (*N* = 460)**	**Non-Charter (*N* = 1,245)**
Satisfied	38	61
Somewhat Satisfied	40	29
Somewhat Dissatisfied	18	8
Dissatisfied	4	2

13. To what extent does the support that Teach For America corps members are provided complement your school's induction and training?

	Percentage of Principals Responding	
Response	**Charter (*N* = 459)**	**Non-Charter (*N* = 1,243)**
To a Great Extent	20	36
To Some Extent	48	45
To a Limited Extent	27	15
Not at All	5	4

14. How many full-time equivalent teachers are in your school?

	Percentage of Principals Responding	
Response	**Charter (*N* = 458)**	**Non-Charter (*N* = 1,237)**
≤10 teachers	27	37
11–20 teachers	22	8
21–30 teachers	22	14
31–40 teachers	14	14
41–50 teachers	7	8
51–60 teachers	4	6
60+ teachers	3	12

15. Are teachers at your school given common planning time (e.g., shared time during the school day in which groups of teachers can plan curricula, review data, or participate in professional development)?

	Percentage of Principals Responding	
Response	**Alumni (*N* = 460)**	**Non-Charter (*N* = 1,245)**
Yes	95	94
No	5	6

16. Is your school . . .

	Percentage of Principals Responding			
	Yes		No	
School Type	**Charter**	**Non-Charter**	**Charter**	**Non-Charter**
A Charter School (*N* = 1,705)	100	0	0	100
A Private School (*N* = 1,653)	1	1	99	99
An Early Childhood Education Center (*N* = 1,651)	3	5	97	95
Managed by the Bureau of Indian Education (*N* = 1,652)	0	1	100	99

17. Are any Teach For America alumni currently teaching in your school this current (2014–2015) school year?

	Percentage of Principals Responding	
Response	**Charter (*N* = 459)**	**Non-Charter (*N* = 1,244)**
Yes	73	48
No	25	44
Unsure	2	8

18. If there are Teach For America alumni currently teaching in your school, how many are working in your school this school year?

	Percentage of Principals Responding	
Response	**Charter (*N* = 339)**	**Non-Charter (*N* = 605)**
1–3 alumni	50	79
4–6 alumni	25	16
7–9 alumni	11	3
10+ alumni	14	1

19. In the following, please only consider Teach For America alumni who are teaching in your school for the current (2014–2015) school year. To what extent do you agree with the following statements?

	Percentage of Principals Responding									
	Strongly Disagree		**Disagree**		**Neither Agree nor Disagree**		**Agree**		**Strongly Agree**	
Statement	**Charter (*N* = ~331)**	**Non-Charter (*N* = ~593)**	**Charter (*N* = ~331)**	**Non-Charter (*N* = ~593)**	**Charter (*N* = ~331)**	**Non-Charter (*N* = ~593)**	**Charter (*N* = ~331)**	**Non-Charter (*N* = ~593)**	**Charter (*N* = ~331)**	**Non-Charter (*N* = ~593)**
Teach For America alumni teachers promote a positive, collaborative, professional culture in the school.	1	1	1	2	7	8	38	41	53	48
Teach For America alumni teachers promote strong relationships with the school community (including students and their parents/guardians).	1	1	1	3	10	15	41	40	48	42
Teach For America alumni teachers exert significant leadership, formal or informal, in the school.	2	1	2	4	11	18	32	36	53	41

20. Are you male or female?

	Percentage of Principals Responding	
Gender	**Charter (*N* = 207)**	**Non-Charter (*N* = 1,495)**
Female	62	63
Male	38	37

21. Are you of Hispanic or Latino origin?

	Percentage of Principals Responding	
Response	**Charter (*N* = 207)**	**Non-Charter (*N* = 1,495)**
Yes	12	15
No	88	85

22. What is your race? (Check all that apply.)

	Percentage of Principals Responding	
Race or Ethnicity	**Charter (*N* = 447)**	**Non-Charter (*N* = 1,218)**
White	63	50
Black or African-American	30	41
Asian	3	2
Native Hawaiian or Other Pacific Islander	0	1
American Indian or Alaska Native	1	2
Other	6	7

NOTE: Calculations assume that all blanks for the question reflect a disagreement with the statement provided. The exhibit should be read, "Of the principals of charter schools who responded to this question, 63 percent identify as being white."

23. Are you enrolled in a state- or federally-recognized tribe?

	Percentage of Principals Responding	
Response	**Charter (*N* = 456)**	**Non-Charter (*N* = 1,230)**
Yes	0	2
No	100	98

24. What is your year of birth?

	Percentage of Principals Responding	
Age Calculated, in Years	**Charter (*N* = 447)**	**Non-Charter (*N* = 1,189)**
25–30	11	2
31–40	50	23
41–50	25	45
51–60	9	22
60+	5	7

25. Are you an alumnus/alumna of Teach For America?

	Percentage of Principals Responding	
Response	**Charter (*N* = 457)**	**Non-Charter (*N* = 1,237)**
Yes	34	4
No	66	96

26. PRIOR to this school year, how many years did you serve as the principal of this or any other school?

	Percentage of Principals Responding	
Response	**Charter (*N* = 457)**	**Non-Charter (*N* = 1,232)**
0–5 years	74	59
6–10 years	17	25
11–15 years	6	11
16–20 years	2	3
20+ years	1	2

27. PRIOR to this school year, how many years did you serve as the principal of THIS school?

	Percentage of Principals Responding	
Response	**Charter (*N* = 454)**	**Non-Charter (*N* = 1,230)**
None	23	19
1 year	26	24
2 years	17	16
3 years	12	11
4 years	9	8
5 years	3	4
6 years	2	4
7 years	2	3
8 years	2	3
9 years	1	2
10 years	1	2
11+ years	2	4

28. Have you served in any other school administrative role (e.g., assistant principal, vice principal, dean) of this or any other school?

	Percentage of Principals Responding	
Response	**Charter (*N* = 457)**	**Non-Charter (*N* = 1,237)**
Yes	82	89
No	18	11

29. Before you became a principal, how many years of elementary or secondary teaching experience did you have?

	Percentage of Principals Responding	
Response	**Charter (*N* = 457)**	**Non-Charter (*N* = 1,232)**
0–5 years	42	22
6–10 years	40	39
11–15 years	10	22
16–20 years	5	11
20+ years	3	7

30. Before you became a principal, did you have any management experience outside of the field of education?

	Percentage of Principals Responding	
Response	**Charter (*N* = 456)**	**Non-Charter (*N* = 1,233)**
Yes	41	43
No	59	57

31. On average throughout the school year, what percentage of time do you estimate that you spend on the following tasks in this school? Rough estimates are sufficient. Please write a percentage in each row. Write 0 if none. Responses should add up to 100%.

Internal administrative tasks, including human resource/personnel issues, regulations, reports, school budget

	Percentage of Principals Responding	
Response	**Charter (*N* = 445)**	**Non-Charter (*N* = 1,206)**
≤10 percent of principal's time	26	17
11–20 percent of principal's time	29	30
21–30 percent of principal's time	24	28
31–40 percent of principal's time	13	13
41–50 percent of principal's time	4	8
50+ percent of principal's time	4	4

Curriculum and teaching-related tasks, including teaching, lesson preparation, classroom observations, mentoring teachers

	Percentage of Principals Responding	
Response	**Charter (*N* = 446)**	**Non-Charter (*N* = 1,207)**
≤10 percent of principal's time	7	4
11–20 percent of principal's time	14	13
21–30 percent of principal's time	21	29
31–40 percent of principal's time	24	23
41–50 percent of principal's time	20	18
50+ percent of principal's time	15	13

Student interactions, including discipline and academic guidance

	Percentage of Principals Responding	
Response	**Charter (*N* = 445)**	**Non-Charter (*N* = 1,205)**
≤10 percent of principal's time	22	24
11–20 percent of principal's time	39	38
21–30 percent of principal's time	28	26
31–40 percent of principal's time	8	7
41–50 percent of principal's time	3	4
50+ percent of principal's time	0	1

Parent interactions, including formal and informal interactions

	Percentage of Principals Responding	
Response	**Charter (*N* = 444)**	**Non-Charter (*N* = 1,202)**
≤10 percent of principal's time	54	52
11–20 percent of principal's time	36	37
21–30 percent of principal's time	10	9
31–40 percent of principal's time	0	0
41–50 percent of principal's time	0	0
50+ percent of principal's time	0	1

Other

	Percentage of Principals Responding	
Response	**Charter (*N* = 348)**	**Non-Charter (*N* = 946)**
≤10 percent of principal's time	87	95
11–20 percent of principal's time	8	4
21–30 percent of principal's time	3	1
31–40 percent of principal's time	1	0
41–50 percent of principal's time	0	0
50+ percent of principal's time	0	1

32. How involved are you in making decisions concerning the hiring of new full-time teachers of this school?

	Percentage of Principals Responding	
Response	**Charter (*N* = 453)**	**Non-Charter (*N* = 1,231)**
No Involvement	0	1
Minor Involvement	1	1
Moderate Involvement	4	5
Major Involvement	95	93

33. Do you participate in interviewing Teach For America corps members?

	Percentage of Principals Responding	
Response	**Charter (*N* = 453)**	**Non-Charter (*N* = 1,228)**
Yes	90	79
No	10	21

References

Baruch, Yehuda, "Response Rate in Academic Studies: A Comparative Analysis," *Human Relations*, Vol. 52, No. 4, April 1999, pp. 421–438.

Baruch, Yehuda, and Brooks C. Holtom, "Survey Response Rate Levels and Trends in Organizational Research," *Human Relations*, Vol. 61, No. 8, August 2008, pp. 1139–1160.

Benjamini, Yoav, and Yosef Hochberg, "Controlling the False Discovery Rate: A Practical and Powerful Approach to Multiple Testing," *Journal of the Royal Statistical Society*, Series B: *Methodological*, Vol. 57, No. 1, 1995, pp. 285–300.

Cook, Colleen, Fred Heath, and Russel L. Thompson, "A Meta-Analysis of Response Rates in Web- or Internet-Based Surveys," *Educational and Psychological Measurement*, Vol. 60, No. 6, December 2000, pp. 821–836.

McCann, Colleen E., Tandra T. Turner, and Richard N. White, *Results from the Teach for America 2013 National Principal Survey*, Washington, D.C.: Teach for America, May 2013. As of August 10, 2015: https://www.teachforamerica.org/sites/default/files/mccann_turner_white_2013_full_report.pdf

National Center for Education Statistics, "Fast Facts: Charter Schools," undated; referenced June 29, 2015. As of August 10, 2015: https://nces.ed.gov/fastfacts/display.asp?id=30

———, "PowerStats: Schools and Staffing Survey, Public and Private School Principals: 2011–12 (SASS Principals 2012)," February 6, 2014. As of August 10, 2015: http://nces.ed.gov/datalab/powerstats/pdf/sass12princombined_subject.pdf

NCES—*See* National Center for Education Statistics.

Rose, Dale S., Stuart D. Sidle, and Kristin H. Griffith, "A Penny for Your Thoughts: Monetary Incentives Improve Response Rates for Company-Sponsored Employee Surveys," *Organizational Research Methods*, Vol. 10, No. 2, April 2007, pp. 225–240.

Teach For America, "About Us," undated; referenced May 18, 2015. As of August 10, 2015: http://www.teachforamerica.org/our-organization

TFA—*See* Teach For America.